# KEY IDEAS IN LAW: T
# AND THE SEPARATION OF POWERS

Prompted by the events following the 2016 referendum on EU member-ship and written during the COVID-19 pandemic by one of the lead-ing public lawyers of our day, this book considers two key constitutional principles, the rule of law and separation of powers, by examining the generality, certainty and predictability of law, relations between the dif-ferent branches of the state, and the mechanisms of accountability within our democracy.

Since the referendum and in the light of the restrictions imposed to deal with the pandemic, and the use of guidelines presented as rules to do so, attention has refocused on the relationship and respective powers and competences of the three branches of the state, the legislature, the execu-tive, and the judiciary. They have also placed strains on our unwritten constitution that have been unknown in modern times.

The role of the courts and of the rule of law has been dramatically illus-trated by recent litigation, most notably the decisions on whether legisla-tion was needed to serve notice of the UK's intention to leave the EU and whether the prorogation of the Westminster Parliament in 2019 was a matter for the courts as opposed to a political question for government.

Set against this backdrop, the book answers the following questions:

- How accessible is the law and how does it avoid arbitrariness?
- How is access to justice protected?
- How does our constitution reflect the separation of powers and the balance of responsibilities between law and politics?
- How does our democracy enable majorities and protect minorities?

**Key Ideas in Law: Volume 3**

## Constitutional Systems of the World

### Series Editor: Nicholas J McBride

Hart Publishing's series *Key Ideas in Law* offers short, stimulating introductions to legal subjects, providing an opportunity to step back from the detail of the law to consider its broader intellectual foundations and ideas, and how these work in practice.

Written by leading legal scholars with great expertise and depth of knowledge, these books offer an unparalleled combination of accessibility, concision, intellectual breadth and originality in legal writing.

Each volume will appeal to students seeking a concise introduction to a subject, stimulating wider reading for a course or deeper understanding for an exam, as well as to scholars and practitioners for the fresh perspectives and new ideas they provide.

### Recent titles in this series:

Key Ideas in Contract Law
*Nicholas J McBride*

Key Ideas in Tort Law
*Peter Cane*

Key Ideas in Law: The Rule of Law and the Separation of Powers
*Jack Beatson*

### For the complete list of titles in this series, see 'Key Ideas in Law' link at www.bloomsburyprofessional.com/uk/series/key-ideas-in-law/

# Key Ideas in Law:
# The Rule of Law and
# the Separation of Powers

Jack Beatson

·HART·

OXFORD · LONDON · NEW YORK · NEW DELHI · SYDNEY

HART PUBLISHING

Bloomsbury Publishing Plc

Kemp House, Chawley Park, Cumnor Hill, Oxford, OX2 9PH, UK

1385 Broadway, New York, NY 10018, USA

29 Earlsfort Terrace, Dublin 2, Ireland

HART PUBLISHING, the Hart/Stag logo, BLOOMSBURY and the Diana logo are
trademarks of Bloomsbury Publishing Plc

First published in Great Britain 2021

Reprinted 2023

A catalogue record for this book is available from the British Library.

Library of Congress Cataloging-in-Publication data

Names: Beatson, Jack, 1948- author.

Title: Key ideas in Law: the rule of law and the separation of powers / Jack Beatson.

Description: Oxford, UK ; New York, NY : Hart Publishing, an imprint of Bloomsbury Publishing,
2021. | Series: Key ideas in law ; volume 3 | Includes bibliographical references and index.

Identifiers: LCCN 2021011705 (print) | LCCN 2021011706 (ebook) |
ISBN 9781509938773 (paperback) | ISBN 9781509938803 (pdf) |
ISBN 9781509938780 (Epub)

Subjects: LCSH: Rule of law. | Separation of powers.

Classification: LCC K3171 .B425 2021 (print) | LCC K3171 (ebook) | DDC 340/.11—dc23

LC record available at https://lccn.loc.gov/2021011705

LC ebook record available at https://lccn.loc.gov/2021011706

ISBN:    PB:      978-1-50993-877-3
         ePDF:    978-1-50993-880-3
         ePub:    978-1-50993-878-0

Typeset by Compuscript Ltd, Shannon
Printed and bound in Great Britain by CPI Group (UK) Ltd, Croydon CR0 4YY

To find out more about our authors and books visit www.hartpublishing.co.uk. Here you will find extracts,
author information, details of forthcoming events and the option to sign up for our newsletters.

"The evidence Beatson marshals – of constitutional strains unprecedented in modern times ... – is sufficiently troubling to merit for his book a wider audience than the students, scholars and practitioners of law for whom it is principally intended ... By explaining the mechanical underpinnings of the largely invisible vehicle that we call our constitution, Beatson has written a valuable manual for anyone who needs to keep it running or who simply wishes to discharge a civic duty by seeking to comprehend it." – *David Anderson, Literary Review*

"This book is notable for the precision and acumen with which topics that are still much debated in English judicial culture are treated, such as that of constitutional law, still considered a fragile category; that of Dicey's theses on the 'Rule of Law'; that of the historical component in the evolution of British law; that of the clarity of laws, on which the author distinguishes a realist approach from a 'romantic' approach; and that of global and supranational law." – *Sabino Cassese, Il Sole 24 Ore (Bloomsbury translation)*

# CONTENTS

# 1

## Overview

Although the United Kingdom does not have a single document entitled 'The Constitution', it nevertheless possesses a Constitution, established over the course of our history by common law, statutes, conventions and practice. Since it has not been codified, it has developed pragmatically, and remains sufficiently flexible to be capable of further development

*R (Miller) v The Prime Minister & Cherry v Advocate General for Scotland* [2019] UKSC 41, at [39].

This book deals with the way the principles of the rule of law and separation of powers work in the British constitution. This chapter provides an introduction to the two principles and to the fuller discussion in later chapters. It also outlines our sources of law, constitutional framework and the constitutional renewal that has taken place since 1997.

The United Kingdom ('UK') is a state with three separate common law systems of law or jurisdictions. They are those of England and Wales (although there is now a debate about the creation of a separate Welsh jurisdiction), Scotland and Northern Ireland. They operate within complex institutional structures resulting from the asymmetric and evolving devolution of legislative and executive power to Northern Ireland since 1922 and to Scotland and Wales since 1998 following referendums. There are important differences between the three legal systems. But in relation to the rule of law and the separation of powers, because, as Loughlin 2013 at 20[1] observed, 'the spirit informing the British constitution is exemplified in the English legal tradition', and in order not to misrepresent

---

[1] Full references to books, articles, Parliamentary reports and cases referred to in the text can be found by consulting the Bibliography and Table of Cases at the back of the book. Numbers on their own are to pages; numbers prefixed by § or §§ are to paragraphs or sections, and a year is included if there are references to more than one item by an author or Parliamentary Committee.

Scottish or Northern Irish law, the focus of this book is on their operation in the law of England and Wales.

# I. THE RULE OF LAW

The rule of law has a long history, according to some stretching back
to Aristotle. The modern UK principle is rooted in the nineteenth century and AV Dicey's 1885 *Introduction to the Law of the Constitution*
('Dicey'), discussed in chapter three. As Dicey recognised, the breadth
and open-textured nature of the principle carries a degree of uncertainty and vagueness. This is something not addressed by section 1 of
the Constitutional Reform Act 2005 ('CRA'), which refers to 'the existing
constitutional principle of the rule of law' without any indication as to
its content or source. Judges are therefore left to decide what it means
in particular cases. They do so by having regard to the ideas of generality, certainty and the prospectivity and predictability of legal norms that
have underpinned the principle. The importance of the principle has led
for example to the rejection of the view expressed in *Shaw v DPP* [1962]
AC 222, in the context of conspiracy to corrupt public morals, that courts
have a residual power to declare acts to be criminal offences, see 42.

The rule of law is also at the heart of many international instruments,
the first of which was the Universal Declaration of Human Rights in
1948. For the UK the most directly relevant is the European Convention
on Human Rights 1950 ('ECHR'). The Human Rights Act 1998 ('HRA')
has given effect to the ECHR in the UK's domestic law by a new, indirect
form of incorporation which, although arguably incomplete, in practice
makes Convention rights generally enforceable. The importance of the
rule of law to the ECHR is shown by the many references to it in
the jurisprudence of the European Court of Human Rights (the
'Strasbourg Court') which must be taken into account by UK courts, but
which is persuasive rather than binding: HRA, section 2(1).

At the core of the rule of law principle is acceptance that the law binds
everybody, including the government. The government must be able to
point to a valid legal basis for its conduct in statute, prerogative powers
enjoyed by the monarch or her ministers, or under the general common
law. The law must also be both impartial and applied impartially, and all

should have access to its protection. 'Nobody is above the law and nobody is outside the law': Steyn 2006, 246.

The position at common law today is that, particularly in relation to fundamental rights such as personal liberty, 'every person within the jurisdiction enjoys the equal protection of our laws': *Khawaja v Home Secretary* [1984] AC 74, at 111 *per* Lord Scarman. This, and the common law principle that like cases be treated alike (see *Matadeen v Pointu* [1999] 1 AC 98, 109), are now complemented and enhanced by the requirements of the ECHR, including the principle of non-discrimination.

The principle of equality, and the need for cogent reasons for departing from it, were major factors in the decision in *Ghaidan v Godin-Mendoza* [2004] UKHL 30 that legislation giving opposite-sex partners but not same-sex ones the right to succeed to a tenancy was incompatible with Convention rights. The principle of non-discrimination was also important in *A v Home Secretary* [2004] UKHL 56 ('the Belmarsh case') where the House of Lords held that legislation authorising the detention without trial of foreign citizens suspected of being terrorists, but not of British citizens so suspected, was also incompatible with Convention rights.

This equality and impartiality do not mean that all laws must apply equally to everyone. There may be different provision for different categories of people according to economic or social conditions or professional or other status. For example, there are financial thresholds for entitlement to welfare benefits and the different tax bands. Sections 24 and 24A of the Police and Criminal Evidence Act 1984 give police officers more extensive powers of arrest without a warrant than members of the public have. But officials also need to be subjected to restrictions which enable them to be accountable. What must be avoided are irrelevant or irrational distinctions, such as linking employability to the colour of a person's hair or skin.

The virtue of the rule of law principle is that it enables individuals, associations and officials to conduct their lives in a lawful manner and to know that they will have a remedy against those who do not. The corollary is that it provides protection and a remedy against unlawfulness and against arbitrary and harsh conduct by government and others including prosecuting authorities.

It has recently been argued (for example by Endicott in Tomkins and Scott, 123, 128–29) that public authorities, including the government, have undefined open-ended inherent powers to carry out their own responsibilities for the public good and to do anything that serves the purposes for which they exist unless such power is taken away by law. Undoubtedly the government needs to be able to exercise executive power effectively and efficiently but the dominant and better view is that a public authority must be able to point to a valid legal basis for its conduct in statute, common law or, in the case of central government, prerogative power. In *R v Somerset CC, ex p Fewings* [1995] 1 All ER 513, 524, a successful challenge to a local authority's ban on stag hunting on its land, Laws J stated that:

> a public body has no heritage of legal rights which it enjoys for its own sake; at every turn, all of its dealings constitute the fulfilment of duties which it owes to others; indeed, it exists for no other purpose. ... it has no rights of its own, no axe to grind beyond its public responsibility.

On appeal, Bingham LJ stated ([1995] 1 WLR 1037, 1042) that it 'is not lawful for you to do anything save what the law expressly or impliedly authorises. ... There are legal limits to every power you have'. This chimes with decisions such as *BBC v Johns* [1965] Ch 32 where the BBC unsuccessfully argued that it was entitled to the Crown's immunity from general taxation because it was a body set up by royal charter. Diplock LJ stated at 79 that it was '350 years and a civil war too late for the Queen's courts to broaden the prerogative. The limits within which the executive government may impose obligations or restraints on citizens are now well settled and incapable of extension'.

The defenders of the idea of public authorities having power to carry out their own responsibilities unless it has been taken away by law say that this treats them in the same way as private individuals and produces symmetry of principle. However, that ignores the imbalance of power between public authorities and almost all private citizens and companies. It also undermines the idea of residual liberties allowing citizens to do all that is not prohibited because recognising that the state and possibly other public authorities have such open-ended inherent powers, save where expressly taken away by law, could remove such liberties. Thirdly, it significantly discounts the uncertainty that would result from open-ended inherent powers and the practical difficulty that would be caused by leaving it to the citizen to find the law which removes the power to act in a particular case. For these reasons, even a purely formal concept of the rule of law requires that the executive should have legal authority for the action it takes in the public interest and that it should not act in breach of the law: Ewing and Gearty 394.

While what has been said is primarily directed at the conception applicable in domestic law, the underlying ideas and virtues of the rule of law principle also apply to the system of international law and the behaviour of states. But although, by and large, states comply with international law, there are obstacles to attaining the ideals of the rule of law in the international legal order: Crawford 2014, §460. One is the absence of a centralised legislative power and the consequent need for many decisions to be made by consensus if they are to be made at all. A second is that enforcement systems, such as that of the International Court of Justice, depend on the consent of states. A third is that political calculations may lead to a willingness to break international law. A recent example is the Internal Market Bill 2020 where the UK government proposed to give itself power unilaterally to rewrite and breach elements of the withdrawal agreement with the EU, a treaty binding the UK under international law and given effect in UK law by the EU (Withdrawal Agreement) Act 2020. The attempt was very widely criticised on rule of law grounds and, after the clauses were rejected by the House of Lords, they were dropped by the government.

## II. THE SEPARATION OF POWERS

The idea that there should be a separation of the powers of the state can also be traced back to Aristotle but was developed by Locke and Montesquieu in the seventeenth and eighteenth centuries. Broadly described, it is the view that the legislative, executive and judicial powers and functions of the state should be carried out independently of each other so that there is a system of checks and balances between the three which restrains tyranny and the abuse of power. Those who make or who administer the law should not determine whether an individual has broken that law. That should be done by an independent and impartial judge.

The CRA sought to make a distinct constitutional separation between the judiciary and the legislature and executive by removing the final court of appeal from the House of Lords and removing the Lord

Chancellor, a senior government minister, from the role of Head of the Judiciary: see 11. But, save for the independence of the judiciary and the power of the courts to supervise the legality of the acts of government and other public bodies by judicial review, the separation of powers has not been recognised as a constitutional principle. The functions of the legislature and the executive are closely related. Ministers are also members of Parliament and, save in the rare case of a 'hung' Parliament, a coalition or a minority government, or acute internal divisions within the majority party, the executive controls the House of Commons. And, since the Parliament Act 1911 the House of Lords has had no veto over legislation, only a delaying power shortened by the Parliament Act 1949 to one year or, in the case of money bills, one month, the executive generally controls the legislative process. Our institutional arrangements and the principle of Parliamentary sovereignty have therefore created what Lord Hailsham, 25–32, described as an 'elective dictatorship', albeit one democratically accountable to the electorate at general elections, and, in the last 50 years in referendums, such as those on membership of the European Community (now the EU) in 1975 and 2016, and on devolution.

We shall see in later chapters that the exercise by the courts of their supervisory jurisdiction by judicial review shows sensitivity to which questions are appropriate for a court and which should be left to the legislature and the executive. In this way they show an appreciation of the separation of powers. Some critics, however, notably supporters of the Judicial Power Project, consider that insufficient sensitivity has been shown in recent years, believing that there has been judicial overreach which has produced a rule of judges rather than a rule of law.

# III. THE CONSTITUTIONAL FRAMEWORK

The foundational principle of the constitution is the sovereignty of the UK Parliament at Westminster. This sovereignty means that Parliament is competent to make or unmake any law on any topic and the courts are required to give effect to those laws. Under the classical model of the UK's constitution there are thus no legal limits on what Parliament may do by primary legislation, including altering the period between general elections and amending or repealing legislation protecting individual rights, such as the HRA. Some consider such legal sovereignty to be incompatible with the rule of law, and there are certainly tensions between the two, and between it and the principle of separation of powers. The way the courts have resolved these tensions will be seen in the discussion of their approach in later chapters. Dicey sought to resolve them by constitutional conventions, that is by political rather than legal controls.

Some Scottish lawyers consider that 'the principle of the unlimited sovereignty of parliament is a distinctively English principle which has no counterpart in Scottish constitutional law': Lord Cooper in *MacCormick v Lord Advocate* 1953 SC 396 411–12, and see Lord Hope in *Jackson v Attorney General* [2005] UKHL 56 at [106]. For them, the Act of Union with Scotland 1706 is a higher form of law which may prevail over inconsistent statutes of the UK Parliament. But, short of extreme situations involving derogations from positions protected by the Act of Union, Scottish courts have been reluctant to claim a power to review the validity of a statute of the UK Parliament: *MacCormick v Lord Advocate* at 413; *Gibson v Lord Advocate* 1975 SLT 134.

There are also tensions between the representative nature of our democracy, which is reflected in the principle of Parliamentary sovereignty, and the development of referendums and the power of the electorate under the Recall of MPs Act 2015, to trigger a special election to remove their MP before the end of his or her term. These developments, which give an enhanced role to direct democracy and may require some re-evaluation of the idea that ours is a representative democracy, are beyond the scope of this book.

It has been said that 'since 1832 constitutional revision in Britain has almost exclusively been the work of governments anxious, first and foremost, to broaden the basis of consent for the executive': Adonis, at 278. This is true of the main components of the UK's constitutional renewal since 1997, devolution and the enactment of the HRA mentioned earlier. The UK statutes establishing devolved unicameral legislatures and executives limit their competence by reserving certain matters called 'devolution issues' to the UK Parliament and by providing that it is beyond the powers of the devolved legislatures to do anything which is incompatible with rights under the ECHR. The courts are expressly given jurisdiction to determine whether the non-sovereign devolved legislatures have acted within their competence on these matters. Sections 3 and 4 of the HRA have made the ECHR and its values part of our domestic law, except where the UK Parliament has unequivocally legislated to the contrary.

These major constitutional measures have resulted in renewed interest in the rule of law and the separation of powers.

In the HRA, Parliament sought to reconcile the enhanced effect given in domestic law to the rights under the ECHR with Parliamentary sovereignty. It did so by the powerful interpretive requirement in section 3 which obliges courts to read legislation in a Convention-compatible way where 'it is possible to do so', but not permitting them to override legislation that cannot be read in a compatible way. In such cases, section 4 preserves the sovereignty of Parliament and its role by providing that courts are limited to declaring that legislation is incompatible with a Convention right, which, see 126–7 and 135–6, leaves it to Parliament to decide whether to amend or repeal incompatible legislation.

The force of the interpretative obligation in section 3 is seen from *Ghaidan v Godin-Mendoza* [2004] UKHL 30 in which the same-sex partner of a statutory tenant was held entitled to succeed to the tenancy although the conventional interpretation of the provision in the Rent Act 1977 treated survivors of same-sex partnerships less favourably than survivors of opposite-sex partnerships. Lord Nicholls stated that section 3 'may require a court to depart from the unambiguous meaning the legislation would otherwise bear' provided the meaning is not 'inconsistent with a fundamental feature of [the] legislation'. That, he stated, would 'cross the constitutional boundary section 3 seeks to demarcate and preserve'. In such a case, as exemplified by *Bellinger v Bellinger* [2003] UKHL 21 referred to at 126–7, a declaration of incompatibility will be made.

Although devolution and the HRA may in practice have eroded the sovereignty of the UK Parliament, formally and legally it remains. In 2005 Lord Bingham described it as 'the bedrock of the British Constitution' and Lord Steyn stated that it is 'the *general* principle of our constitution': see *Jackson v Attorney General* [2005] UKHL 56 respectively at [9] and [102]. See also Bingham 2011, Chapter 12.

The main issue in *Jackson's* case was whether the Hunting Act 2004 banning most forms of hunting with dogs was not primary legislation because it was passed without the consent of the House of Lords using the power under the Parliament Act 1949, an Act itself made under the Parliament Act 1911 and without the consent of the House of Lords. The argument that the 1949 Act was delegated or subordinate legislation and, as such its validity was open to investigation in the courts, was rejected (at [64]) as 'an absurd and confusing mischaracterisation'.

As to wider aspects of sovereignty, Lord Bingham referred at [41] to concerns that the effect of the Parliament Acts 1911 and 1949 has been to erode 'the checks and balances inherent in the British constitution when Crown, Lords and Commons were independent and substantial bases of power, leaving the Commons, dominated by the executive, as the ultimately unconstrained power in the state'. The abolition of the House of Lords' veto on legislation, while justified by its unelected nature, has been an important element in this erosion. The resulting weakness of Parliament in restraining the executive has, however, led to a debate about the nature of Parliamentary sovereignty.

Is, as some consider, sovereignty a construct of the common law created by the judges and which they might have to qualify using techniques with deep historical roots, in the words of Lord Steyn in *Jackson's* case at [102], 'in exceptional circumstances involving an attempt to abolish judicial review or the ordinary role of the courts'? A similar view was taken by three members of the Supreme Court in *R (Privacy International) v Investigatory Powers Tribunal* [2019] UKSC 22 at [144]. Or was sovereignty created by Parliament's victory in the English Civil War in the seventeenth century, the political reality of which was then accepted by the courts? For that reason, Lord Bingham 2011, at 168 considered that Parliament might legislate in a way which infringed the principles of the rule of law if it did so very clearly.

Lord Bingham rejected the argument that the courts could modify the principle of Parliamentary sovereignty because he did not regard it as just a common law rule but as the rule of recognition which is the ultimate foundation of our entire legal system. He considered that as such it cannot and should not be altered by judges because that would mean that an undemocratic part of the state took power from the democratic and accountable parts in an undemocratic way. The erosion of the checks and balances referred to by Lord Bingham strengthens the case for change and there are strong arguments that any change should be by legislation, and probably then only after a referendum. But, perhaps not surprisingly, constitutional reforms initiated by governments have ducked the issue.

Leaving aside the case of legislation seeking to exclude access to the ordinary courts, discussed at 139 and 144, the courts are likely to regard any modification of the sovereignty of the UK Parliament as a matter for our elected representatives. In *Re the UK Withdrawal from the EU (Legal Continuity) (Scotland) Bill* [2018] UKSC 64, in the context of the devolution settlement, the Supreme Court affirmed a muscular version of this sovereignty. It held that the Scottish Parliament did not have power to legislate for the repatriation of powers that had been governed by EU law in accordance with the division of competencies in the devolution legislation because an Act of the UK Parliament, the EU (Withdrawal) Act 2018, made provision for all powers to be repatriated to the UK rather than to Scotland. The court stated (at [11]) that whether devolved or UK institutions would acquire those competencies involved 'questions of policy, which are the responsibility of our elected representatives and in which the wider civil society has an interest'. What is striking is that the court accepted the power of the UK Parliament unilaterally to modify the devolution settlement or at least the way it worked in practice and declined to assume an expansive constitutional role. The centrality of parliamentary sovereignty, particularly its importance in ensuring the political accountability of the executive, is also seen from the decisions discussed at 12–13.

Although not stated to be a devolution issue, whether an enactment of a devolved legislature is within its competence is amenable to the common law supervisory jurisdiction of the courts, albeit with a need for some circumspection in the light of the democratic mandates of those legislatures: see *AXA General Insurance Co Ltd v Lord Advocate* [2011] UKSC 46 at [47]–[49], [51] and [153]–[154]. Lord Hope adapted the approach he and Lord Steyn took in *Jackson's* case. He stated of legislation 'to abolish judicial review or to diminish the role of the courts in protecting the interests of the individual', that 'the rule of law requires that the judges must retain the power to insist that legislation of that extreme kind is not law which the courts will recognise'. Lord Reed considered that in enacting the devolution statutes, the UK Parliament did not legislate in a vacuum but 'for a liberal democracy founded on particular constitutional principles and traditions'. He concluded: '[t]hat being so, Parliament cannot be taken to have intended to establish a body which was free to abrogate fundamental rights or to violate the rule of law'.

Another reason for the renewed interest in the rule of law and the separation of powers concerns the position of the judiciary. The independence of the judiciary has been a cornerstone of the British constitution since the Act of Settlement 1701. From the 1980s courts have linked it to the separation of powers. Sir John Donaldson MR stated that the separation and independence of the judicial and legislative powers was 'a constitutional convention of the highest importance': *R v HM Treasury, ex p Smedley* [1985] QB 657, 666. In *R v Home Secretary, ex p Fire Brigades Union* [1995] 2 AC 513, at 567 Lord Mustill put it more broadly:

> It is a feature of the peculiarly British conception of the separation of powers that Parliament, the executive and the courts each have their distinct and largely exclusive domain. Parliament has a legally unchallengeable right to make whatever laws it thinks fit. The executive carries on the administration of the country in accordance with the powers conferred on it by law. The courts interpret the laws and see that they are obeyed.

The effective incorporation of Article 6 of the ECHR into domestic law, with its requirement for courts and tribunals to be 'independent and impartial', intensified longstanding criticism of two aspects of our arrangements. One was that the highest court of the land was a committee of the House of Lords and thus part of the legislature. The second was that the head of the judiciary of England and Wales was the Lord Chancellor, a senior government minister and member and Speaker of the House of Lords, who also appointed judges and from time to time presided in appeals in the House of Lords. In Scotland, there was a similar multiplicity of functions. The Lord Advocate combined the roles of being a member of the government (before devolution the UK government), head of the Scottish public prosecution service, and the appointer of judges. The concept of separation of powers underlying these criticisms led to further reform.

In June 2003, without prior consultation, it was announced that the office of Lord Chancellor was abolished and that a Supreme Court of the United Kingdom and a Judicial Appointments Commission would be created. Ultimately the office was not abolished but fundamentally reformed so that its holder was no longer the head of the judiciary of England and Wales or a judge. The process involved negotiations with the judiciary culminating first in an agreement, 'the Concordat', reallocating all functions exercised by the Lord Chancellor in a judicial capacity to the Lord Chief Justice, and later the CRA 2005. Judges were given a larger and more formal role in the administration of the court system and the headship of the judiciary of England and Wales passed to the Lord Chief Justice. For a lively account of the background to what the House of Commons Constitutional Affairs Committee 2004 at §§ 14, 189 described as the 'hurried' and 'over-hasty' way this fundamental reform was introduced see Reynold, 1–33. See also Gee, Hazell, Malleson and O'Brien, 37. In Scotland, similar reforms were made by the Judiciary and Courts (Scotland) Act 2008.

A third factor in generating renewed interest in the principles has been litigation on sensitive issues concerning individuals such as the beginning and end of life, sexuality and restrictions on personal liberty arising from the state's response to terrorism. The shape of such litigation and the approach of the courts is in part the result of the role which Parliament, by enacting the HRA, assigned to the courts. It is, however, important to remember that its roots go deeper. They lie in the growth of judicial review in the second half of the twentieth century, and in particular since the 1960s, when significant decisions of the House of Lords developed the principles of procedural fairness and legality. The UK Supreme Court has considered whether it is for the courts, as opposed to Parliament, to determine whether there should be a legal status for same sex couples. In *Ghaidan v Godin-Mendoza* [2004] UKHL 30 it decided that it was. It has also considered whether it is for the courts to determine whether assisted suicide should be lawful, and, if so, on what conditions. In *R (Nicklinson) v Ministry of Justice* [2014] UKSC 38 discussed at 127 it decided (albeit giving a variety of reasons) that this was an issue for legislation by Parliament rather than for the courts. Four years later, in *R (Conway) v Secretary of State for Justice* [2018] UKSC B1 the Supreme Court refused to consider a further appeal on assisted suicide. As a result, in the UK the separation of powers 'means that some areas of life are excluded from judicial decision, and others are protected by the judiciary from invasion by the other two branches of government': Hoffmann 2002, §17. The extent to which this is so is discussed in chapter eight.

The fourth factor was the litigation in 2017 and 2019 following the UK's Referendum on EU membership in 2016. The experience after the 2017 election of having a government without a majority in the House of Commons refocussed attention on the relationship and respective powers and competences of the three branches of the state, the legislature, the executive and the judiciary, and the relationship between UK and devolved institutions.

In *R (Miller) v Secretary of State for Exiting the EU* [2017] UKSC 5 ('*Miller 1*'), a majority of the UK Supreme Court decided that legislation was required in order to serve notice of the UK's intention to leave the EU under Article 50 of the EU Treaty. The Court also held that the constitutional conventions which govern the way Dicey reconciled Parliamentary sovereignty and the rule of law are not justiciable. Accordingly, the Sewel convention that the UK Parliament would not normally legislate about devolved matters except with the agreement of the devolved legislature is a political convention which, see *Miller 1* at [136]–[137], courts do not enforce. Although now enshrined in section 28(8) of the Scotland Act 1998, and section 107(6) of the Government of Wales Act 2006, the purpose of those provisions was not to convert the convention into an enforceable legal rule but only 'to entrench it as a convention': *Miller 1* at [148]–[149].

In *R (Miller) v The Prime Minister & Cherry v Advocate General for Scotland* [2019] UKSC 41 ('*Miller 2 & Cherry*') the Supreme Court unanimously decided that the Prime Minister's decision to advise the Queen to prorogue the UK Parliament in 2019 was a matter for the courts and not just a political question for government, and that the 2019 prorogation was not lawful. This attempted use of the prerogative power to prorogue in this way is notable because it was an attempt by the executive to bypass any legislative control of it at a crucial time in the period immediately before the UK's withdrawal from the EU. The Court explained at [45]–[47] that parliamentary sovereignty matters to our constitution because it is required to ensure the political accountability of the executive and thus to protect citizens from the arbitrary exercise of power.

These issues engaged not only the 'usual suspects', lawyers, politicians, political scientists, journalists and scholars, but also the wider public which followed and was engaged by the legal cases and debates and votes in Parliament. For an insightful and accessible account of what happened and the wider context, see Rozenberg, especially chapters 2 and 12. Serving and recently retired judges have contributed to the discussion in the media on these and other issues, such as the restrictions imposed as a result of the COVID-19 pandemic. This raises questions about their impartiality and risks damage to the perception that the judiciary is impartial, a fundamental aspect of the principle of judicial independence. The result has been that our unwritten constitution has been subjected to strains previously unknown in modern times which test understanding of the rule of law and separation of powers.

# IV. SOURCES OF LAW

In the domestic law of common law systems there are two sources of 'hard law', legislation and the common law. In Britain, there is no single constitutional instrument. Legislation is enacted by Parliament or under its authority. There is also a third and more controversial quasi-legislative source, sometimes called 'soft law'. To a limited extent, in the way described at 16, international law is also a source of our domestic common law while not being part of it.

Most of our law is now found in legislation. Statutes (primary legislation) are enacted by both Houses of the UK Parliament or the devolved Scottish and Welsh Parliaments and the Northern Ireland Assembly. Secondary, subordinate or delegated legislation in the form of statutory instruments is made by ministers or regulators pursuant to statutory powers, or in Orders in Council made by ministers pursuant to the Crown's non-statutory prerogative and common law powers.

There are some 4,350 Acts of the UK Parliament and 80,530 UK statutory instruments to be found on legislation.gov.uk, the database that has been available since 2006 without charge. Every year between 1950 and 2019 an average of 59 UK statutes and 2,500 UK statutory instruments were passed. A slow decline in the number of statutes over the past 40 years has been outweighed by an increase in delegated legislation, the highwater mark was some 87 per cent of legislation in 2007: HC Library Briefing Paper 2019.

'The reality [is] that statute law is the dominant source of law of our time': Steyn 2003, 5. But, as the examples at 43–45 show, the legal principles developed by the decisions of the courts, particularly appellate courts, remain important sources of law. In that sense they are 'judge-made law'. This law is often referred to as the 'common law', a term which today includes the principles of equity historically developed by the separate courts of Chancery as well as those developed in the common law courts. The rules are generated by courts applying institutional principles of adjudication in individual decisions and exercising a harmonising and formative influence, consciously or unconsciously moulding the law to social conditions: Eisenberg, 154; Allen, CK, 124, 127, 162. The method used is inductive and generally incremental, moving gradually from the particular to the general, but (see 44–45) there can be greater shifts. While statute can supplement or replace the common law, the common law 'provides the residual gapless law where there is no statute'. Accordingly, despite the factual dominance of statutes, 'in a conceptual sense our common law remains the primary source of law': Burrows, 45.

'Soft-law' in the form of administrative rules, guidance and policies may be issued by government or regulatory bodies to specify what others should do or the approach the body itself will take. Guidance by central government might indicate what it expects local authorities to do in the discharge of, for instance, their care and support responsibilities under the Care Act 2014. Similarly, there is guidance from the Home Office about its approach when considering applications by citizens of other countries to enter or to stay in the UK. The decision in *R (Purdy) v DPP* [2009] UKHL 45 required the Crown Prosecution Service to provide guidance about its approach when considering whether to prosecute in sensitive and ethically difficult cases, such as assisted suicide thus promoting accessibility. See further 61–62.

Such guidance is controversial because it is made without the formalities associated with statutes and delegated legislation, but is nevertheless capable of imposing obligations and conferring rights on citizens, or at least 'of influencing how obligations and rights are to be applied or construed': Greenberg 2015, 99. This has been particularly evident in the response to the COVID-19 pandemic, because the boundaries between what the law requires by statute and regulation and the content of government advice to citizens have been blurred. Non-binding guidance, for instance as to when citizens could leave their homes, was more restrictive than the regulations required but government presented it as 'what you can and can't do', seemingly summarising the legal restrictions. Not surprisingly, such government assertions initially led to reports of police seeking to enforce guidance going beyond the regulations: Sandhurst and Speight, 5–7. This is seriously problematic from the perspective of the rule of law and is likely to adversely affect the public's confidence in government and the police. Furthermore, the Joint Committee for Statutory Instruments has stated of the guidance on conduct during the COVID-19 pandemic, 'non-statutory guidance cannot be used to fill gaps in the law, which must be sufficiently clear and certain on its face to enable the individuals to whom it applies to be able to comply with it': 22nd Report of Session 2019–21, § 2.4.

'Soft law' may be statutory, in that it is made pursuant to a direction or a power in a statute, or non-statutory. Although its precise effect will depend on its nature and context, it is generally weaker than legislation and in some cases its status and legal categorisation is unclear or disputed. For example, the Immigration Rules have been said to be 'detailed statements by a minister … as to how the Crown proposes to exercise its discretionary power to control immigration', rather than delegated legislation: *Odelola v Home Secretary* [2009] UKHL 25 at [6], *per* Lord Hoffmann. The Law Commission in 2019 stated at §3.21 that the Immigration Rules should be viewed 'as a unique form of legal text', essentially 'a hybrid of administrative policy and legal rules'. Those rules can be seen as an example of statutory guidance because, although the Immigration Act 1971 does not explicitly empower the Home Secretary to make rules, it provides the statutory machinery for the exercise of the Home Secretary's powers.

A clearer example of statutory guidance is that given by the Secretary of State for Health and Social Care to local authorities about how they should go about performing their care and support responsibilities under the Care Act 2014 and the regulations made under it. Section 78 of the Care Act requires local authorities 'to act under the general guidance of the Secretary of State'. The courts have interpreted such language to mean that local and other public authorities should give 'great weight' to such guidance, and should depart from it only where there are 'good' reasons for doing so but 'without freedom to take a substantially different course': see *R v Islington LBC, ex p. Rixon* (1997–98) 1 CCL Rep 119 at 123. In *R (Munjaz) v Mersey Care NHS Trust* [2005] UKHL 58 at [20] Lord Bingham said that 'there is a categorical difference between guidance and instruction'.

International law derives from two sources: treaties entered into by states, and custom established by the general practice of States and their acceptance that such practice reflects or amounts to law. A treaty entered into by the UK is an executive act which binds it under international law but 'is not part of English law unless and until it has been incorporated into the law by legislation': *Rayner JH (Mincing Lane) v Department of Trade and Industry* [1990] 2 AC 418, 500. But the common law is open to influence from international law. Customary international law is a source of UK domestic law on which judges can and should draw unless barred by statute or domestic constitutional principle: *Keyu v Foreign Secretary* [2015] UKSC 69 at [10]; *R (Freedom and Justice Party) v Foreign Secretary* [2016] EWHC 2010 (Admin) at [166]. Also, a presumption that Parliament does not intend to act in breach of international law means that treaties and treaty-based standards concerning human rights may be used to resolve an ambiguity in a statute, as an aid to the development of the common law, and as a guide to public policy: for detailed discussion see Crawford 2019,§§ 59–67 and 71. Moreover, even though unincorporated treaties are not part of UK domestic law, government ministers are duty bound to comply with international law as part of their overarching duty under the Ministerial Code to 'comply with the law': *R (Gulf Centre for Human Rights) v Prime Minister* [2018] EWCA Civ 1855 at [22]–[23].

# 2

# Formal and Substantive Conceptions of the Rule of Law

There are essentially two conceptions of the rule of law. One, a formal concept, is that the rule of law is concerned with how the law is made and applied and not with its content: Raz 1977. The other is that it is also about the substantive content of the law which must conform to certain fundamental values or substantive ideals: Dworkin, 11–12.

Adherents of both conceptions have a spectrum of approaches, so the distinction between the two conceptions is in practice not binary. Both attach importance to the values of reasonable accessibility and clarity, relative stability, impartiality and prospective rather than retrospective application of law. Ideally these values require a framework of general rules to be laid down in advance. A simple example is that individuals should know what the speed limit is on any road. The value of impartiality and the separation of powers mean that whether an individual has exceeded the speed limit and broken the law should be determined by an independent judge.

The key aspect of the formal conception of the rule of law is that its adherents consider that those values suffice. For them, a legal system in an undemocratic state or in a democratic state which for example permits inequalities based on race, gender or religion, and is to that extent unjust, could nevertheless in principle conform to the rule of law if its rules and principles are clear, prospective and publicly accessible: see for example Raz 1977, 211 and 221. A purely formal conception of the rule of law does not require a Bill of Rights because it only aims to eliminate the kinds of arbitrary governmental power which can unfairly upset citizens' expectations about their legal obligations and rights: Goldsworthy, 63–64. Even tyrannical laws, and the abhorrent apartheid laws in South Africa before 1994 where peoples' rights depended on their race, might satisfy the formal concept. This is not because its adherents are indifferent to the content of the law. It is because they consider that the rule of law is only one of the virtues to which the law should conform. For them, other principles, such as fairness and equality, are independent ideals which are needed for the law to be good or just, and the rule of law should not be used to explain those principles.

It is important to bear in mind that there are different degrees to which the values of accessibility, clarity and prospectivity are achievable. For example, although the extent to which discretion in a particular context is either desirable or cannot be avoided is controversial, many adherents of the formal concept now accept that certainty and clarity may have to be qualified. It is recognised that those exercising governmental powers in a modern state need some discretion in order to avoid the disadvantages of 'legalism'. Moreover, where law is dealing with complex technical, medical or scientific issues, there is a limit to the ability of those making it, whether legislators or judges, to produce language that will be fully understood by laypeople.

The substantive conception of the rule of law regards law as more than simply what is enacted by the legislature or other state body with the requisite authority, according to the designated procedure, and scrupulously observed by state officials and others implementing it. It is concerned with the content of the law and its values and ideals, and requires, in the words of Sir John Laws 2021 at 19 that the law 'be imbued with certain norms, standards or principles' to protect the individual citizen's autonomy and to constrain 'the power of government, including democratic government'. One simple example of such substantive values is the presumption of innocence which protects a person charged with a crime and requires the prosecution to prove beyond reasonable doubt that that person is guilty. Referred to as 'the golden thread' running through the common law, the approach of the courts to statutory provisions qualifying or restricting it is discussed below at 85. The approach to another value, that of respect for private property rights which protects the right to own and not to be arbitrarily deprived of property without legal authority and without compensation, is discussed at 46, 65 and 140.

A more complex illustration of this substantive conception is the United Nations' formulation of the rule of law on its website as:

> a principle of governance in which all persons, institutions and entities, public and private, including the State itself, are accountable to laws that are publicly promulgated, equally enforced and independently adjudicated, and which are

consistent with international human rights norms and standards. It requires measures to ensure adherence to the principles of supremacy of the law, equality before the law, accountability to the law, fairness in the application of the law, separation of powers, participation in decision-making, legal certainty, avoidance of arbitrariness, and procedural and legal transparency.

Those who favour a conception with a substantive dimension recognise that complying with the values reflected in the formal conception gives some protection because 'even in the most perverted regimes there is a certain hesitancy about writing cruelties, intolerances and inhumanities into law': Fuller, 637. But, while they see that protection as necessary, they regard it as partial and contingent.

> [A] tyranny devoted to pernicious ends has no self-sufficient reason to submit itself to the discipline of operating consistently through the demanding processes of law, granted that the rational point of such self-discipline is the very value of reciprocity, fairness, and respect for persons which the tyrant ex hypothesis, holds in contempt: Finnis, 373.

Some adherents of the formal conception, including Joseph Raz, consider that those who favour a conception with a substantive dimension are using the term 'rule of law' to express several distinct and diverse principles such as democracy and fundamental human rights as well as the principles and values in the first conception. They consider that the result is to risk mistakenly ascribing a single rationale or similar importance to those principles and the principles embodied in the formal conception of the rule of law: Raz 1977, 196. Taken to extremes, the result would be one of two undesirable consequences. The first is that the rule of law would involve the identification of a complete social or political philosophy leaving no independent function for the conception of the rule of law. The second is that it would become one of those self-congratulatory and conclusory rhetorical devices or idioms, like motherhood and apple-pie, a synonym for what is 'good', the meaning of which is shot through with uncertainty: Shklar, 1.

The uncertainty is reflected in the fact that there are legitimate differences of view as to what values or ideals are fundamental and should be required, and those differences are carried into this conception of the rule of law. Uncertainty also arises because, even where it is recognised that a right, for example the right to a fair trial, is fundamental and absolute, it is accepted that different states may give effect to it in different ways: Lord Bingham in *Brown v Stott* [2003] 1 AC 681, at 702.

As to what rights are fundamental, some stress the importance of property rights and the market; others point to individual human rights such as the right not to be subjected to torture or inhuman treatment, to freedom of religion, liberty and equality; and others to public interest and community rights. Carrying these differences into a conception of the rule of law means that its formulation will be either controversial or so general and vacuous as to be unhelpful save as a vague aspiration.

A general principle of respect for private property rights, with no more, might be seen as a worthy aspiration. But deciding which rights qualify as property rights, for instance whether information, rights under contracts, and entitlements to work in a profession or trade qualify is likely to be controversial and to depend on the law-maker's political position. So is formulating the extent to which of the rights recognised as property rights are fundamental and must be secured. The conditions under which individual rights may be interfered with in the general public interest, for example, in order to build a hospital, a road or an airport, or to deal with a pandemic, and the question of compensation for such interference are also likely to be controversial. Interference with such individual rights and values in the interest of those of the wider community is typically a decision for the democratically accountable institutions of the state: see 66–67 and 126–29.

Some of those who favour a conception of the rule of law with a substantive dimension consider that the formal conception is a mask deployed to legitimise substantive inequalities: Unger, 176–81, 192–223. Others consider that adherents of the formal conception give insufficient weight to the fact that their focus on clarity, prospectivity and accessibility is not enough. They reject making a hard distinction between the formal and the substantive on the ground that the formal conception is itself based on substantive foundations such as moral autonomy and individual respect, and that the application of principles as well as rules is necessary and cannot exclude substantive factors. They recognise that the formal conception can achieve 'precision and coherence' and has the advantage of 'definitional certainty' but claim the price of these is 'a somewhat impractical detachment' which is not suitable for practical decision-making: Allan 1993, 20–21, 26–28. Allan regards the rule of law as primarily an ideal of procedural fairness but one which also has important implications for the permissible content of laws and policies: Allan 2001, 1 and Allan 2013, 100.

Lord Bingham recognised the logical force of the distinction between the content of the law and the way it is enacted. But he considered that

> a state which savagely represses or persecutes sections of its people cannot …
> be regarded as observing the rule of law, even if the transport of the persecuted
> minority to the concentration camp or the compulsory exposure of female
> children on the mountainside is the subject of detailed laws duly enacted and
> scrupulously observed: Bingham 2011, 67.

How then to escape from a conception of the rule of law which requires the identification of a complete social or political philosophy? One might look, for example, to international instruments such as the Universal Declaration of Human Rights and the ECHR which protect the equality and dignity of individuals and have already started to shape the development of the international rule of law: Crawford 2014, §§488–89.

For Sir John Laws 2021, 17–19 and 23, the formal conception, which he calls 'the thin theory' is 'more than it seems' because the independent and impartial mechanism for law enforcement applies objective standards lying beyond the unqualified interests of the legislator and which import constitutional norms reflecting the values of the system. He points to the statement of Dicey set out at the end of the next chapter. The constitutional norms and values relied on by our system are discussed in chapters four to nine.

# 3

# Dicey's Rule of Law and the Twentieth-Century Critiques

The major influences on the understanding of the rule of law in the UK are the accounts in Dicey's *An Introduction to the Law of the Constitution* in 1885, and the twentieth-century critiques of him, most recently that in 2011 by Lord Bingham. Dicey attempted to reconcile the principles of the rule of law and the fact that Parliament is sovereign, and can make and unmake any law whatsoever, by stressing the independent position the courts enjoy under the constitution: Dicey 1885, 413–14 set out below at 28. But his analysis did not reflect the reality of our constitution at the end of the nineteenth century and, as the twentieth century progressed, it became even less valid.

Dicey did not find reconciliation between the principles of the rule of law and parliamentary sovereignty in the operation of constitutional conventions. He stated that conventions are not rules of law which will be enforced in the courts. They are generally rules for determining the exercise of the prerogative by the executive to ensure that Parliament gives effect to the will of what he regarded as the true political sovereign, the majority of the electors: Dicey 1885, 24, 429, 439–40. By 1914 he had revised his position to the extent of recognising that although not rules of law, conventions are obeyed 'by the force of law' because breaches of convention would almost immediately lead to conflict with the law and the courts: Dicey 1885, 445–46. The flaw, as ECS Wade observed in his introduction to the tenth edition, is that it is possible to enact a convention in statutory form and yet exclude it from enforcement in the court: Dicey 1885, xxix. *Miller 1* discussed at 12 and 124–5 is a striking modern illustration of the fact that a convention is not justiciable and enforceable in the courts even if, as the Sewel convention in that case was, it is enshrined in statute.

Many consider that the twentieth-century critiques mean that Dicey's approach no longer warrants detailed analysis: see for example De Smith, at 30. But the way it, and the responses to it, have shaped our understanding of the rule of law means that a brief summary of both remains a useful backdrop to the discussion in the other chapters of this book.

Dicey recognised that the terms 'rule of law', 'government of law' and 'supremacy of law' are full of vagueness and ambiguity. He sought to deal with this by stating that, when applied to the British constitution, the terms have three meanings. They are:

## 1. Supremacy of Regular Law Established in Ordinary Courts as Opposed to Arbitrary Discretionary Power

No man is punishable or can lawfully be made to suffer in body or goods except for a distinct breach of law established in the ordinary legal manner before the ordinary courts of the land. (188)

Dicey later summarised this first meaning in the following words:

[The rule of law] means ... the absolute supremacy or predominance of regular law as opposed to the influence of arbitrary power, and excludes the existence of arbitrariness, of prerogative, or even of wide discretionary authority on the part of the government. (202)

## 2. Equal Subjection of All to the Ordinary Law of the State and the Jurisdiction of the Ordinary Courts, and No Exceptional Powers to State Officials

Dicey stated that:

[n]o man is above the law, [and] (what is a different thing) ... every man, whatever be his rank or condition, is subject to the ordinary law of the realm and amenable to the jurisdiction of the ordinary tribunals. (193)

His later summary of this was that the rule of law means:

equality before the law, or the equal subjection of all classes to the ordinary law of the land administered by the ordinary law courts; the 'rule of law' in this sense excludes the idea of any exemption of officials or others from the duty of obedience to the law which governs other citizens or from the jurisdiction of the ordinary tribunals. (202–03)

## 3. The General Principles of the Constitution are the Result of Judicial Decisions Determining the Rights of Private Persons in Particular Cases Brought Before the Courts and Not a Written Constitution

[T]he constitution is pervaded by the rule of law on the ground that the general principles of the constitution (as for example the right to personal

liberty, or the right of public meeting) are with us as the result of judicial decisions determining the rights of private persons in particular cases brought
before the courts; whereas under many foreign constitutions the security (such
as it is) given to the rights of individuals results, or appears to result, from the
general principles of the constitution. (195–96)

The main elements of the twentieth-century critique of each of these
three meanings of the rule of law in the British constitution, from those
by Sir Ivor Jennings 1933 and William Robson 1928 to the more recent
ones such as those by Craig 1990, Loughlin 1992, Bingham 2011, and
Sedley 2015, chapter 14, can be summarised as follows:

- The first meaning reflects Dicey's failure to recognise the existence
  of the discretionary power which existed in his day or to consider the
  legal limitations on such power. Discretionary power became much
  more pervasive during the twentieth century as the modern state
  (to a greater or lesser extent) regulated the economy and provided
  social services. These involved the delegation to ministers and officials of wide powers including the ability to make policy choices
  limited only by an increasingly skeletal legislative framework. The
  consequence is that Dicey's analysis, always incomplete, is now even
  less comprehensive.

- As to the second meaning, it may be the case today that no individual
  or official is above the law, and no one should be penalised save for
  a breach of the law. But when Dicey 1885 stated (at 202–03) that the
  principle 'excludes the idea of any exemption of officials or others
  from the duty of obedience to the law which governs other citizens',
  he grossly underestimated the problems of a British citizen seeking redress against the government even in private law matters: see
  Bingham 2002, 51. Many of the impediments were only removed by
  the Crown Proceedings Act 1947, which first sought to subject ministers and government departments to the rules of liability governing
  citizens and non-governmental entities. Even then, some differences
  remained, notably the prohibition of injunctive relief against the
  Crown in civil proceedings. It was only in 1993 that it was held that
  injunctions could be granted against ministers and other officers of
  the Crown in judicial review proceedings: *M v Home Office* [1994]
  1 AC 377.

- The second meaning also overlooked the fact that statute and prerogative give governmental and other bodies powers that private individuals do not have, such as the right to arrest, to enter property, and to regulate business and professional conduct. 'All are equally subject to the law, though the law to which some are subject may be different from the law to which others are subject': Wright 1945, 4.

- The first and second meanings also reflect Dicey's focus on individual liberty, property rights and personal private law rights arising from breaches of contracts, as a result of civil wrongs ('torts'), or as a result of the defendant's unjust enrichment. They fail to address the differences between the role of the courts in determining the merits of disputes between private persons and entities about such private law matters, and their more limited supervisory role over the acts and omissions of governmental and other public bodies. They thus fail to take account of administrative law even as it was during Dicey's life.

- The third meaning neglects the extent to which rights are given by legislation and qualified by legislation.

- More fundamentally, the third meaning is difficult to reconcile both with a purely formal interpretation of Dicey's account and with the sovereignty of Parliament, the other pillar of Dicey's analysis: see Craig 1997, 470 and Allan 2001, 13 & 20, and 2013, 102–104. That sovereignty means, as Lord Bingham 2011 at 168 accepted, that legislation incompatible with, for example, personal liberty and freedom of expression can be enacted and, unless insufficiently clear, must be enforced by the courts, even if retrospective. As explained earlier, Dicey saw the limits on Parliamentary sovereignty as conventional, that is ultimately political rather than legal. This was even so for common law rights such as rights of access to a court, not to be imprisoned save by the law of the land, to property, and to freedom of expression, the first two having their origins in clauses 33 and 40 of the Magna Carta of 1215. They were regarded as important in his time and are today often described as common law constitutional rights and are among the rights protected by the ECHR and the HRA.

For Lord Bingham (see 174) the rule of law is an ideal worth striving for to secure good governance, rather than a fixed set of principles. But he accepted that Parliament can legislate in a way that infringes its principles.

Despite his concern at the way the checks and balances in the constitution have been undermined by the rise in executive power, he rejected the argument that in exceptional circumstances the courts could modify the principle of Parliamentary sovereignty, see chapter one at 9. His critique of the formal conception of the rule of law is discussed in chapter two at 20–21. His analysis also sought to address the criticism that the principles as stated by Dicey and others were too uncertain. He did so by identifying the ingredients of the over-arching and otherwise over-general principle more precisely. He considered that those ingredients included the following eight sub-principles:

(1) The law must be accessible and so far as possible intelligible, clear and predictable.

(2) Questions of legal right and liability should ordinarily be resolved by application of the law and not the exercise of discretion.

(3) The laws of the land should apply equally to all, save to the extent that objective differences justify differentiation.

(4) Ministers and public officers at all levels must exercise the powers conferred on them in good faith, fairly, for the purpose for which the powers were conferred, without exceeding the limits of such powers, and not unreasonably.

(5) The law must afford adequate protection of fundamental human rights.

(6) Means must be provided for resolving, without prohibitive cost or inordinate delay, bona fide civil disputes which the parties themselves are unable to resolve.

(7) Adjudicative procedures provided by the state should be fair.

(8) The rule of law requires compliance by the state with its obligations in international law as in national law.

Lord Bingham accepted that others would come up with different principles or would, as I seek to do in the remainder of this book, express them differently.

For Sir John Laws 2021, at 16, Lord Bingham's list of substantive requirements 'are, in truth, a suggested list of the virtues of a decent nation', but the list 'fails to capture the distinct quality or characteristic which the law – the Rule of Law – provides or contributes'. He considered Lord Bingham's statement, set out above at 21, as just 'an assertion'. For Sir John, the distinct quality or characteristic is the independent and impartial mechanism for law enforcement, applying objective standards.

The difference may reflect a difference between an analysis heavily influenced by the evidence of history, as Lord Bingham's is, and one heavily influenced by philosophy, as Sir John Laws's is. Both are important in understanding our position today. Sir John invokes implicit support by Dicey 1885, who at 413–14, stated:

> Parliament is supreme legislator, but from the moment Parliament has uttered its will as lawgiver, that will becomes subject to the interpretation put upon it by the judges ... who are influenced ... by the general spirit of the common law, are disposed to construe statutory exceptions to common law principles in a mode which would not commend itself either to a body of officials, or to the Houses of Parliament, if the Houses were called upon to interpret their own enactments.

Notwithstanding the powerful critique of Dicey's approach, we shall see that this part of what he said chimes with the approach of courts to the principles of procedural fairness and legality mentioned in chapter one and discussed at 34 and 83–95 and in chapters five, eight and nine.

# 4

## Accessibility of Law

To be able to comply with the law, individuals, companies, officials and public bodies must know or be able to find out what is required, and what their rights and duties are. Otherwise the law will not be capable of guiding their behaviour. Where a provision restricts a person's rights under the ECHR, it must be 'prescribed by' or 'in accordance with' law, which means that it must be accessible in the sense that the individual or entity has an adequate indication of the legal rules applicable to a given case and that it is formulated with sufficient precision to enable them to regulate their conduct: *Sunday Times v UK* (1979) 2 EHRR 245 at [49]. There are thus two overlapping components, accessibility and reasonable certainty.

This chapter considers how the rule of law values of certainty and predictability are protected by requiring law to be accessible to ordinary individuals or their advisers before they commit themselves to a course of action. Accessibility can be broken down into four components: publication, clarity and intelligibility, a large degree of prospectivity, and reasonable stability. These components do not operate identically for the different sources of law discussed at 13–16. As there is a close link between accessibility and the principle of open justice whereby court hearings and decisions must generally be in public, and information about the court system, their volumes of work and costs should be accessible, this chapter also deals with that principle.

The key factor in the accessibility of law is the ability to find out what the law requires. In some cases, there will be a general awareness of what is required even if not of the detail. Most people know that assault and theft are criminal offences. But they may not know that assault includes any conduct which intentionally or recklessly causes another person to apprehend immediate and unlawful personal violence, or how courts have interpreted the requirements of intention and recklessness. They may also not know that, under section 1(1) of the Theft Act 1968, a person is only guilty of theft 'if he dishonestly appropriates property belonging to another with the intention of permanently depriving the other of it', what the concept of 'appropriation' involves or how courts have interpreted the requirement of 'dishonesty'. For the answer to the last question, see 40.

Moreover, the law on any topic is not generally to be found in a single source. It is spread over numerous statutes, statutory instruments and decisions of the courts which may have to be read together to ascertain the answer to the problem at hand. The legislation on firearms and immigration are good examples of the dispersal of the law. In 2017 it was estimated that there were some 34 pieces of legislation on firearms spread over 100 years, and about a dozen Acts on immigration since the Immigration Act 1971. In the decade after 1997 some 55 Acts of Parliament altered the rules of criminal justice: HL Constitution Committee 2017, §137, Evidence QQ 103, 107 and Spencer 2008.

These examples demonstrate that the complexity of law means that for most people accessibility requires access to advice, whether from a lawyer, an advice centre, an association such as a professional or trade interest group or trade union, or an NGO such as the Child Poverty Action Group, RSPCA, or Liberty. The need for such advice is not inimical to the rule of law, although its unavailability might be, see 81. It is therefore important that there is an independent legal profession with a duty to represent clients, including those with unpopular or odious views and those charged with heinous crimes, within an overriding duty to act with integrity and uphold the rule of law and the administration of justice. Invidious attacks by government identifying lawyers working in particular fields with the alleged sins of their clients undermines the rule of law and may prevent effective access to justice. This is not an activity confined to one political party: see O'Nions and Fouzder.

# I. PUBLICATION

All primary and secondary legislation is published, the latter identifying the statutory source of the power under which it is made. Since 2006 government has also made primary and secondary legislation available online through legislation.gov.uk. Statutes from 1801 are on the database, the vast majority now in a revised form and up to date or are stated not to be. It is possible to use a 'timeline of changes' feature to see how statutes have changed or (if an amendment is not yet in force) could change over time. A complete dataset of the original version of secondary legislation from 1987 is available, although only some from 2018 has been revised. While government must be entitled to react swiftly to emergencies, in order effectively to let people know what they can and they cannot do, restrictions which interfere with family and private life and the ability to earn one's livelihood should not come into effect before or very shortly after the legal instrument is published. This, however, has been the case for many regulations made to deal with the COVID 19 pandemic.

Until relatively recently, government was content to leave it to commercial publishers to produce up to date versions of legislation. The position has changed since the digital revolution, but it is still not possible to search all legislation on legislation.gov.uk by subject-matter. Even if all the relevant legislation is identified and found, to get the answer may also require access to decisions of the courts interpreting the statutory words or expounding the common law. Accordingly, although legislation is published, these factors may impede full accessibility, even disregarding the questions of clarity, intelligibility, stability and certainty considered below.

As to the common law, a legal system which recognises the decisions of courts as a source of law depends on the availability of those decisions. Law reporting developed haphazardly from the late-thirteenth century Year Books and the mid-sixteenth century summaries of advocates' arguments and judgments published in 'nominate' reports by or attributed to well-known lawyers. For about 150 years, a series published by the Incorporated Council of Law Reporting ('ICLR'), a legal charity covering the work of the Appellate Courts and the High Court, has been regarded as the 'Official Law Reports'. It also publishes a weekly generalist series, and specialist series on employment law, business law, and public and third sector law. Additionally, many commercial series deal with specialised areas such as personal injuries, local government, shipping, and insurance.

Less than approximately two per cent of decisions are published in 'hard copy' reports. The ICLR seeks to filter out the many cases which raise issues of fact and not law, and only to report decisions which lay down a new rule or principle of law, change or clarify the existing law, provide an interpretation of a legislative provision, or are an important illustration of a new application of accepted principles. Commercial series also report cases on matters such as the interpretation of terms in standard form contracts and the application of principles within their area of specialisation.

Over the last 40 years cases have become available and searchable on the web. At first this was through commercial legal information systems such as Lexis and Westlaw. Since 2000 the British and Irish Legal Information Institute ('BAILII'), a charitable trust, provides free access to 102 databases covering 10 UK and foreign jurisdictions. During 2019 BAILII received almost 12 million visits and uploaded almost 37,000 judgments and other materials. While in some ways not as sophisticated as the commercial systems, BAILII publishes the great majority of decisions in the senior courts and many cases in the appellate criminal courts.

As in the case of legislation, widespread publication at no cost does not mean that the decisions of the courts are fully accessible. Susskind 2008, at 261 stated that 'databases of statutes and cases will not do this job for citizens'. He correctly observed that people need tools which actually help in their own precise circumstances rather than which point to potentially relevant legal sources and which may result in 'information overload'. More recently he has advocated an online triage system embedded in publicly funded court and tribunal systems, to identify the nature of a problem, the legal issue, and alternatives to litigation. He accepts that publicly funded systems do not have the resources for this, and that it will be provided by commercial entities and, he hopes, charitable and educational bodies: Susskind 2019 Ch 11, 2020, 12.

Soft law is published more informally and is sometimes not published at all: *R (Lumba) v Home Secretary* [2011] UKSC 12. When published, while searchable online, the source of the power to make it is not always clear and it may be difficult to ascertain whether one has found the relevant version of the document. The elusive way in which policy emerges from statutory guidance may also mean that it is not clearly published and does not meet the required standards of transparency and clarity: *R (Detention Action) v Home Secretary* [2014] EWCA Civ 1634 at [58] and [70]. Moreover, while the informal language of soft law may make it easier for non-lawyers to understand, it may obscure any tension or incompatibility between its language and the language of the legislative instruments and the decisions of the courts which are of greater weight in the legal hierarchy. In the case of the Immigration Rules, the more informal language has not prevented lack of clarity or 'a degree of complexity which even the Byzantine Emperors would have envied': *Pokhriyal v Home Secretary* [2013] EWCA Civ 1568 at [4] and Law Commission (2020) §§1.6–1.9.

# II. CLARITY AND INTELLIGIBILITY

In 2013 the head of the Office of Parliamentary Counsel ('OPC'), the office responsible for drafting all government bills, said that users of the law regard it as 'intricate and intimidating': OPC 2013A. That year the OPC launched a 'Good Law' initiative, the latest of many initiatives to make legislation more accessible and understandable for UK citizens. Its aim was to improve the clarity and coherence of legislation, to ensure it is necessary, and, where possible, to simplify it, while recognising that some complexity is unavoidable 'in a complicated world in which law is used to balance competing interests': OPC 2013B.

Commendable progress has been made, but, given the amount of existing legislation and the volume of new legislation each year, the process will be slow. The House of Lords ('HL') Constitution Committee stated (2017A, §3) that it is evident

> that there remain large bodies of law which are remarkably inaccessible and difficult for practitioners to comprehend, let alone the average citizen. Quite aside from the obvious rule of law concerns that arise, such law leads to costly and unnecessary strains on the resources of the justice system.

Legislation is drafted, for the most part, to lay down general rules although some is highly specific. Its clarity is affected by several factors, notably length and complexity and the style of drafting. Legislators may seek to achieve clarity in one of two ways, which one former First Parliamentary Counsel described as 'realist' and 'romantic' approaches.

The realist approach is the dominant style of drafting in the UK. The drafter seeks to address all that a legislative instrument is to cover in a very detailed way and to provide answers to all scenarios and circumstances. The text may at first sight be difficult to understand because of the level of detail and the complexity of language used to achieve greater precision, but the claim is that, albeit with some effort, the 'realist' approach to drafting will provide a clear answer, at least to skilled lawyers.

The romantic approach frames legislation more generally and deploys its underlying principles as 'broad general rules': Renton Committee, recommendation 13. It is generally easier to read and to be clear or at least appear clear about the answers to the main issues addressed by it. Where the answer is not linguistically clear from the words, perhaps because the legislation has to be applied to circumstances that were completely unforeseeable at the time it was enacted, it should be possible to determine it by reference to those underlying principles. For example, when it is not clear whether legislation restricts a fundamental right or value such as personal liberty or freedom of speech, the courts will have recourse to a general 'principle of legality'. In *R v Home Secretary, ex p Simms* [2000] 2 AC 115, 131 Lord Hoffmann stated that 'the principle of legality means that Parliament must squarely confront what it is doing and accept the political cost. Fundamental rights cannot be overridden by general or ambiguous words'. Absent 'express language or necessary implication to the contrary, the courts therefore presume that even the most general words were intended to be subject to the basic rights of the individual'.

Critics of the realist approach maintain that it is needlessly complicated, and that clarity is not promoted by it. So, for example, tax legislation has been criticised for inconsistency in the terms and definitions used: see HL Constitution Committee, 2017A, § 104. Also, the fact that, as noted above, the law on any topic is not generally in a single piece of legislation and answers to questions may require recourse to decisions of the courts is an impediment to clarity.

There are similar problems with some statutes dealing with criminal law. The sentencing provisions in the Criminal Justice Act 2003 were described in *Lang* [2005] EWCA Crim. 2864 at [16] and [153] as 'labyrinthine' and 'astonishingly complex'. In *R (Noone) v Governor of HMP Drake Hall* [2010] UKSC 30 at [87] the amount of intellectual effort, public time and resources to discover a route through the 'legislative morass' to what should be the simplest and more certain of questions, a prisoner's release date, was said to be 'outrageous'. The Sexual Offences Act 2003 has been said to create 'far more criminal offences than are really necessary to achieve its intended aims'. Simester and Sullivan unfavourably compare its 29 sections creating 21 separate offences with the 1996 modernisation of the Italian Penal Code's provisions on non-consensual sex and sexual abuse of minors in nine articles creating four criminal offences. The level of detail in the Sexual Offences Act 2003 was accompanied by a failure to make transitional provisions to deal with the situation where the prosecution is unable to prove whether the defendant's conduct took place before or after it came into effect. The prosecution asked the court to deal with this problem in *A (Prosecutor's Appeal)* [2006] 1 Cr App R 28 but the court considered that further legislation was required. The problem was solved by section 55 of the Violent Crime Reduction Act 2006.

Critics of the romantic approach claim that the legislation may not provide a clear answer or any answer at all to questions that arise during the life of the statute. The consequence is that either the statute will have to be amended or the determination of the answer is left to the judges. But the history of statutory offences of fraud since the Theft Act 1968 shows that this problem can also arise where the legislation is detailed.

The Theft Act 1968 reflected a legislative decision to have a specific series of fraud offences rather than a single general offence of fraud. One reason was that it was considered that specific offences would give more precise guidance as to what conduct was criminal compared to a broad offence. One of the specific offences was dishonestly obtaining 'property belonging to another' by deception contrary to section 15. 'Property' included intangible property such as a person's right to sue another. But in *Preddy* [1996] AC 815, where a borrower dishonestly caused a transfer from a lender's bank account to his own account by deception, the House of Lords identified a lacuna in section 15. This was because the lender's right of property in the sum transferred, which was a right of action against his bank, was extinguished by the transfer. The consequent credit balance in the dishonest borrower's account was therefore a new right of action against the dishonest borrower's own bank which had never belonged to anyone but him and so was not 'property belonging to another' within section 15. As a result, it was necessary to create a new statutory offence of obtaining a money transfer by deception. Despite that, the law of criminal fraud remained in a complicated and fragmented state. Other unmeritorious technical points continued to be taken until the enactment by the Fraud Act 2006 of a general fraud offence.

The criticisms of both approaches show that neither can guarantee certainty. Drafters have to respect the values of our legal system and courts have to draw on those values to resolve questions left open by the bare language of the statute.

The OPC acknowledge that the volume of legislation, the level of detail and the pace and method of changes to legislation make it hard to understand and difficult to comply with: OPC 2013B. Changes in economic conditions and technical, scientific or financial developments mean that legislation becomes out of date and change becomes necessary. Similarly, a change of government which leads to a change of policy will lead to further legislation. But avoidable problems of clarity arise from the way legislation and 'soft law' is amended, the frequency of change in areas such as criminal justice and sentencing, immigration and tax law, the increasing use of multi-purpose (or 'Christmas Tree') statutes such as the Legal Aid, Sentencing and Punishment of Offenders Act 2012 ('LASPO 2012'), and the notable decline in consolidation.

Until relatively recently it was common to make changes by a cross-reference in the later legislation ('referential legislation') rather than a textual amendment to the original legislation. That made it necessary for the reader to pursue what might be 'a long paper-chase through a series of legislative provisions': Bingham 2011, 41. This has changed. For some time, the vast majority of changes to primary legislation have been by textual amendments: see Burrows, 110. For instance, the 2012 and 2013 statutes on self-defence referred to below used textual changes to the 2008 Act. Major changes made by secondary legislation as part of the withdrawal from the EU have, however, been made in a fragmented and referential way.

Consolidation enables complex areas of the law covered by different legislation to be gathered together in one statute. Change without periodic recourse to statutory consolidation adds to fragmentation and the overall lack of clarity. Between 1965, when the Law Commission was founded, and the end of 2006, over 200 consolidation Acts were passed. In the period since then there have been only two. This is regrettable. It is to be hoped that the two consolidation exercises by the Law Commission in 2018 on sentencing law which is now before Parliament and, in 2020, on the soft-law Immigration Rules, will encourage a return to a rolling programme of consolidation. Once an area is consolidated, the availability of the up-to-date version of statutes on the legislation.gov.uk website means the law would be more accessible to lawyers and the general public: see HL Constitution Committee 2017A, §145.

Context is a further factor. The ultimate user of legislation, whether a lay citizen, a member of a profession or trade, or an organisation, should ideally have the capacity to understand it. Intelligibility is of particular importance in legislation on the criminal law because it is 'a particularly public and visible part of the law' which controls the freedom of citizens to act as they wish by state coercion and punishment and also because of the direct role of non-specialist laypeople in its application when serving on juries: Law Commission 1989 §2.5 and 1992 §1.6 and HL Constitution Committee 2017A, §109. However, 'some parts of the criminal law will always, necessarily, be difficult' (Law Commission 1992 §1.4) and, more generally, the precision necessary in legislation on complex technical, scientific or financial matters, or on sensitive ethical questions may mean that it can only be intelligible to those with some expertise in the area.

The coherence and clarity of the underlying policy, and the extent to which it has been affected by the need for political compromise or other constraints, are, as the HL Constitution Committee, 2017A, §14 noted, also important factors. One example is legislation enacted to give a wider defence to householders who use force against a burglar or other criminal who has entered their house. After a prolonged public and political debate and much media support, the requirement that any force in self-defence be 'reasonable' was replaced by a requirement that it not be 'grossly disproportionate': see section 76 of the Criminal Justice and Immigration Act 2008 as amended by sections 148 of LASPO 2012 and section 43 of the Crime and Courts Act 2013. Clarity was not, however, achieved because the status of 'unreasonable' but not 'grossly disproportionate' force was left in the air. The Crown Prosecution Service took the view that a conviction was not realistic in such a case, but the Divisional Court and the Court of Appeal Criminal Division disagreed. They held that the reasonableness standard was preserved, and 'the use of disproportionate force which is short of grossly disproportionate is not, on the wording of the section, of itself necessarily the use of reasonable force': *Ray* [2017] EWCA Crim. 1391 at [26] and *R (Collins) v Secretary of State for Justice* [2016] EWHC 33 (Admin) at [32]–[33].

The problems may be greater where policy and legislation have been developed and enacted in a very short time either because of exigencies of the Parliamentary timetable, or in response to a public outcry. The Dangerous Dogs Act 1991 is a singular example. It was passed within two days of its first reading using a 'fast track' procedure following several well-publicised serious injuries caused by pit bulls and similar dogs which led to demands for swift action. Prohibited dogs including those 'of the type known as the pit bull terrier', or which appeared to the Secretary of State to have the characteristics of a type 'bred for fighting' were to be seized and destroyed. However, the Act left considerable scope for argument about whether a dog was of the specified 'type'. When the public mood changed, further pressure led to amendments to the legislation in 1997, 2014 and 2015 repealing the blanket prohibition based on breed and taking into account the dog's conduct and the owner's fitness. That, however, introduced further uncertainty and litigation has proliferated: see for example *Webb v Chief Constable of Somerset* [2017] EWHC 3311 (Admin).

Clarity is also impeded where legislation is enacted where there is no real need for it or it is for purposes other than changing the law. Legislation should not be used to declare what the common law is or to send out signals for 'aspirational' purposes. Section 1 of the Compensation Act 2006 and the Social Action and Heroism Act 2015 are two examples of unnecessary or largely unnecessary legislation. They were designed to send a 'signal' to dampen down personal injury claims brought as part of what was seen as a 'compensation culture'. Section 1 of the 2006 Act requires courts considering whether a person has been negligent, or to have broken a statutory duty, to have regard to whether a requirement to take steps to meet a standard of care would prevent or discourage a desirable activity being undertaken. But this simply replicates the common law position: *Uren v Corporate Leisure (UK) Ltd* [2011] EWCA Civ 66 at [13]; *Wilkin-Shaw v Fuller* [2012] EWHC 1777 (QB) at [42] affirmed [2013] EWCA Civ 410.

The 2015 Act requires courts considering these questions to have regard to whether the person was acting for the benefit of society, or volunteering, or acting heroically for someone else's benefit. The dominant view is that its provisions also simply replicate the position at common law because courts have been required to take into account the social and economic utility of conduct since at least *Tomlinson v Congleton BC* [2003] UKHL 47 and section 1 of the 2006 Act. Both statutes also introduce unwelcome uncertainty by leaving open the need to consider whether there is a difference (possibly a subtle one which is difficult to determine) between the legislation in question and earlier legislation or the position at common law.

What of the clarity of the common law? Its strength is the way it identifies principles with sufficient certainty to enable citizens, businesses and government to know what is required whilst leaving sufficient room for further incremental development of the law by the courts. Lord Goff stated that he saw the common law 'as a mosaic that is kaleidoscopic in the sense that it is in a constant state of change in minute particulars': Goff, 186. While not irrelevant to clarity and certainty, the implications for the rule of law of possible incremental change and of imprecise substantive standards are considered in the sections on prospectivity at 43 and avoiding arbitrariness at 55. Here the focus is on clarity.

The fact that common-law doctrine is spread over many thousands of cases can impede clarity where, in order to ascertain the law on any point, it is necessary to distil it from many relevant cases. This has led to attempts to codify areas of common law such as the Law Commission's unsuccessful attempts to codify contract and the criminal law over the last 50 years. The reasons those attempts failed included the view that codes were not needed in a jurisdiction with excellent treatises and textbooks doing that distillation, and the belief that legislating common law doctrine could have the effect of freezing the law at a particular point in time: see for example Goff, 173–74, Foskett J in *Uren v Corporate Leisure (UK) Ltd* [2013] EWHC 353 (QB) at [75], and Burrows, 63–67.

It has also been said that 'the length, elaboration and prolixity of some modern common law judgments … can in themselves have the effect of making the law to some extent inaccessible': Bingham 2011, 42–43. There is indeed a sharp contrast between modern judgments and the precise and succinct quality of many nineteenth-century judgments. In some cases, the contrast reflects the multiplicity of factual and legal questions in dispute and the elaborateness of the arguments in modern cases. The contrast may also reflect fashion; the status and almost oracular authority of judges then, and the modern perception that judges must show their path to a result in great detail. They must deal with every point raised or risk being overruled. Length in itself, however, does not generate uncertainty or indicate a lack of clarity in a way inimical to the rule of law, at least to skilled lawyers, but it can be accompanied by factors that do. One is where quotations from earlier judgments are set out sometimes at considerable length without sufficient analysis of their precise relevance.

The existence of inconsistent decisions is another cause of uncertainty. The availability of so many cases on-line and the potential for information overload may mean that a relevant one is not put before the court in a later case, thereby increasing the scope for such inconsistency. But in turn there is also greater scope for inconsistencies to be discovered by an online search and to be resolved by a higher court. The result is a continuing need for the distillations in up to date treatises and textbooks.

The availability of many first instance decisions in specialised areas which are often concerned with resolving what are primarily factual as opposed to legal questions or with the construction of commercial documents may also lead to doctrinal complexity. For instance, a court considering whether a document is a guarantee may have to review a large number of previous decisions with the outcome turning on how near or how far it is from the documents construed in each past case. This can result in fine, sometimes over-refined, distinctions. Longmore LJ, a highly experienced commercial judge, observed that 'the commercial community deserves better than this, if better can be done': *Wuhan Guoyu Logistics Group Co Ltd v Emporiki Bank of Greece SA* [2012] EWCA Civ 1629 at [22].

Where a topic that is not necessary for a decision is addressed, what is said on that topic in a judgment is not binding. It may be influential and sometimes ultimately dispositive, but until the matter is resolved by a later decision there is likely to be some uncertainty. The judgment in *Ivey v Genting Casinos* [2017] UKSC 67 is a striking example. The Supreme Court, after deciding a point of contract law, considered and disapproved the long-standing test for 'dishonesty' in the criminal law which it said should not be followed. It formulated a new objective test which was *obiter* and not binding because it was not necessary for the decision. The position was resolved when, in *Barton & Booth* [2020] EWCA Crim 575, the Court of Appeal Criminal Division stated that it was bound to follow an *obiter* direction by the Supreme Court that an otherwise binding decision of the Court of Appeal should no longer be followed.

Perhaps the most important factor affecting the clarity of common law decisions is that in appellate common law courts there may be multiple judgments. This is more likely where courts are dealing with difficult and complex questions. There appears to be a cyclical pattern to the popularity of single and multiple judgments and, as their respective merits do not really raise 'rule of law' issues, this is not the place to address that question. It suffices to say that a separate judgment, even when concurring in the result, can avoid 'bland generality' in a single judgment which conceals differences between the majority. It can also expose the difficulties of a point and thus lay the foundation for incremental development in the future: Heydon 2013, 210–16. But concurring majority judgments are problematic for certainty where they reach the same conclusion but use different routes or give different emphases. The two examples below show that this may make the identification of what the court as a whole actually decided very difficult.

*Boys v Chaplin* [1971] AC 356 concerned the much-criticised former English rule that where a civil wrong is committed abroad, but the claim is brought in England, the claimant had to show that the defendant (in that case a negligent car driver) was liable both under English law and under the law of the place where the wrong was committed. The House of Lords unanimously decided that the rule was subject to a flexible exception but gave a bewildering variety of different and not consistent routes to the result. The differences included whether the right to claim damages was a substantive or a procedural issue, whether English law or the law of the place where the accident between two British citizens happened was the dominant law, and the role, if any, for a 'proper law' rule enabling the court to choose the law which on policy grounds had the most significant connection with the events. Lord Denning MR suggested that no *ratio* could be extracted: *The Hannah Blumenthal* [1983] 1 AC 854, 873. The ultimate solution to the uncertainty was legislation which abolished the common law rule except in relation to defamation: Private International Law (Miscellaneous Provisions) Act 1995 Part III.

*Belhaj v Straw* [2017] UKSC 3 concerned the foreign act of state doctrine which precludes the sovereign acts of foreign states abroad from being judged in the courts of another state. The Supreme Court held that the doctrine did not bar an English Court from considering claims of UK complicity in abduction and torture by the United States and Libyan authorities. But its 116 pages and 68,336 words of judgments in the Law Reports did not bring clarity. They leave several important points unsettled. Although Mann 1986, 164 described foreign act of state as 'one of the most difficult and most perplexing topics', this is disappointing. There is no clear *ratio*, and there was disagreement as to the types of foreign act of state and their precise scope, for example whether the doctrine applied to wrongs to the person as well as to wrongs against property. Two of the three judges who agreed with Lord Neuberger confined their agreement to his 'reasoning and conclusion'. They stated that Lord Mance had reached the same conclusion for 'essentially' the same reasons, a statement which 'glosses over some not insignificant differences' between Lord Neuberger and Lord Mance, for example as to whether the doctrine is subject to a public policy exception: Simonsen 2017, 952, Smith 2018, 21.

# III. PROSPECTIVITY, RETROSPECTIVITY AND RETROACTIVITY

If the key factor in the accessibility of law is to enable people to know what they can and cannot do, it follows that the law must generally operate prospectively and provide a clear justification where it does not. Prospectivity provides a measure of certainty by protecting the entitlement of individuals to act on the basis of the existing law. As Lord Diplock stated in *Black-Clawson International v Papierwerke Waldhof-Aschaffenberg* [1975] AC 591, 638: '[t]he acceptance of the rule of law as a constitutional principle requires that a citizen, before committing himself to any course of action, should be able to know in advance what are the legal consequences that will flow from it'.

Prospectivity is particularly important in the criminal law. The creation of offences whether by legislation or by the incremental development of the common law which make conduct criminal when it did not contravene the criminal law at the time it took place is prohibited by ECHR Article 7(1) and by the common law: *Knuller v DPP* [1973] AC 435 and *Withers v DPP* [1975] AC 842. Although both decisions rejected the contrary view in *Shaw v DPP* [1962] AC 220 referred to at 2, *Knuller* nevertheless followed the decision in *Shaw* that conspiracy to corrupt public morals is an offence. It did so on the ground that this was required in the interests of certainty of the law. *Withers* was concerned with a charge of conspiracy to effect a public mischief. The House of Lords held that there was no such offence.

Prospectivity is also important in other areas. Businesses and individuals must know or have the means of knowing the lawfulness or the impact of, for example, their liability to tax, or arranging their financial affairs in a particular way. They are entitled to act on the basis of the law in force at that time. They should not, save in exceptional circumstances, find that the law applicable to such past actions which defined their rights and liabilities at that time has subsequently been altered with retroactive effect changing the character and legal consequences of those past actions.

In the case of legislation this aspect of the rule of law is bolstered by the presumption that 'a statute is prospective rather than retrospective in effect unless it distinctly says otherwise': *Docherty* [2016] UKSC 62 at [17] *per* Lord Hughes. While the presumption is an excellent starting point, the discussion below shows that the position is more nuanced. This general maxim does not bring out the distinction between retro-activity and other forms of restrospectivity. It may also not be a reliable guide to what happens in practice because it does not sufficiently reflect the willingness of courts in certain situations to find that the presumption has been rebutted.

Changes to the common law made by decisions of the courts develop-
ing the law in the way described at 14 and 38 appear at first sight to pose a
significant challenge to this aspect of the rule of law. This is because under
the declaratory theory of adjudication 'the law as altered by a decision is
deemed always to have applied, and the previously settled understanding
of the law was treated as a mistake': *Prudential Assurance v Revenue and
Customs* [2018] UKSC 39 at [63]. The effect of such a decision is thus retroactive but outside the criminal law this is not seen as an unacceptable
deviation from the rule of law.

Why is this? One reason is that courts do not generally develop the
common law by entering or re-entering a field regulated by legislation.
To do so would inevitably risk the powers and duties so developed being
inconsistent with those prescribed by Parliament: *Re McKerr* [2004]
1 WLR 807 at [30]. Another reason is that the common law must be
capable of change if it is to be kept relevant to a changing world. A third
is that courts sometimes have no real choice but to develop the common law where a case has identified an apparent lacuna in the law which
needs to be addressed urgently and waiting for legislation is not a practical alternative. In such, a case making law cannot defeat expectations
and in any event the legislature is left with the last word. For instance, as
recently as 1989, the question whether medical treatment could lawfully
be given to an adult who is precluded by mental incapacity from consent-
ing to it revealed a lacuna in legislation and the common law which the
court filled by using the common law principle of necessity: *Re F (Mental
Patient: Sterilisation)* [1990] 2 AC 1, 71–72, 74, 76–77 *per* Lord Goff.

The most important factor, however, in reconciling judicial law-
making with this aspect of the rule of law is that, to preserve legal certainty, judicial development is generally evolutionary and incremental.
The process modestly builds on existing principle and does so within
a general framework of respect for precedent. It acknowledges the
pre-eminent constitutional role of Parliament in making new law and
the procedural and institutional limitations which restrict the ability
of litigation before the courts to act as an engine of law reform. For
instance, in *Elizouli v Home Secretary* [2020] UKSC 10 at [170]–[171]
the Supreme Court considered that to recognise a common law right
that the state should not facilitate a trial in a foreign jurisdiction where
there was a prospect that such a trial would lead to the death penalty
being carried out would be a radical rather than an incremental development and refused to do so.

The result is that the direction of travel of doctrinal development is generally foreseeable. Perhaps the most significant changes to the law made by the courts in the last 70 years have been to the supervisory jurisdiction by judicial review over public authorities. Evolutionary development since the 1950s has widened the scope of this jurisdiction and narrowed the area within which a court will not interfere with a decision of a public authority. Since *Anisminic v Foreign Compensation Commission* [1969] 2 AC 147 discussed at 144 the courts have had a wide power to correct errors of law by administrative bodies, even where the legislation governing the body expressly provided that its decisions 'should not be called in question in any court of law' because such an error deprives the body of the power to make the decision. *Ridge v Baldwin* [1964] AC 40 significantly strengthened the requirement of procedural fairness that an opportunity should be given to the person affected to make representations before a decision is made. The retrospectivity of such decisions has not been seen as problematic where it favours an individual dealing with a public authority. So, in *R v Governor of Brockhill Prison, ex p Evans (No 2)* [2001] 2 AC 19 the statutory period the claimant was to serve in prison was calculated by the prison governor in accordance with authoritative decisions which were overruled after she had been detained for 59 days longer than she should have been on the new interpretation of the statute. The application of retrospectivity to the new interpretation meant that it had been the law at the time she should have been released and she was entitled to damages for false imprisonment.

Where a greater shift in the common law occurs, for example by a court widening an existing offence or creating a new civil liability, there is a clear tension with this aspect of the rule of law and the change has to be within the boundaries set by wider legal principles. It can generally be expected to be based on some general societal consensus that it is appropriate, or to concern a rule that is uncertain or has been eroded by exceptions in previous cases which makes a change foreseeable, at least by those who take advice. This was so in *Donoghue v Stevenson* [1932] AC 562 when the House of Lords synthesised individual categories of liability to establish a broad general principle requiring manufacturers of consumer goods to take reasonable care for the health and safety of the consumers of those goods. It was also the case when it abolished the common law immunity of a husband to a charge of raping his wife in *R v R* [1992] 1 AC 599, 623 and when it set aside the rule that money paid under a mistake of law was not generally recoverable by a claim for restitution in *Kleinwort Benson v Lincoln CC* [1999] 2 AC 349. Those two rules were subject to many exceptions which called into question their coherence. The recognition of a category of civil liability based on the defendant's unjust enrichment that was subject to a defence of change of position also removed the justification for barring recovery of payments under a mistake of law.

Nevertheless, there may be consequential problems. In *Kleinwort Benson* the court recognised that retrospectivity could unduly harm the public interest in security of transactions because there would be many claims arising from mistaken payments of tax in the distant past. This was because the Revenue was liable to pay interest from the date of the payments but the limitation period for the taxpayer to make a claim did not start running until much later when it was discovered that the tax was not due. The court considered that problem could be addressed by legislation changing the limitation period in such cases. It, however, later turned out that it could not be because limitation periods with retrospective effect were held to be incompatible with EU law: *Prudential Assurance v Revenue and Customs* at [60]–[64]. Ultimately the matter was resolved by holding that time began to run when a claimant could with reasonable diligence and advice have discovered his mistake in the sense of recognising that a worthwhile claim arose rather than the later date on which an authoritative appellate judgment so held: *Test Claimants in the FII Group v HMRC* [2020] UKSC 47 at [209]–[213].

Returning to the case of legislative change, Parliamentary sovereignty means that in principle there is no limit to the power of Parliament to legislate. The presumption that legislation is not retroactive is constitutionally important in a similar way to the principle of legality discussed at 34 and 141. It is a means of ensuring that if retrospectivity is desired, Parliament squarely confronts what it is doing and accepts the political cost.

General statements of the presumption have been said to use the term '"retrospective" to describe a range of different effects, some more and some less extreme': *Wilson v First County Trust Ltd (No 2)* [2003] UKHL 40 at [186] *per* Lord Rodger. At one extreme is legislation which alters the substantive law applicable to events and transactions that occurred before it came into force. Because such provisions actually affect the position before the legislation came into force, they can be called 'retroactive'. The presumption is that statute speaks only to the future and that Parliament did not intend to speak to the past in a manner which is unfair to those concerned, unless a contrary intention is expressly or by necessary implication required by the language of the statute.

A striking example of expressly retroactive legislation is the War Damage Act 1965. It overturned the decision of the House of Lords in *Burmah Oil Co v Lord Advocate* [1965] AC 75 that, save for 'battle damage', compensation was payable for damage to property caused by lawful acts of the Crown during war. Such legislation, although consistent with the principle that Parliament is sovereign, is problematic for this aspect of the rule of law. Today, unless justified, damage to or deprivation of property without compensation would be contrary to Article 1 of Protocol 1 of the ECHR. A more recent example is that the power of the Treasury under the Banking Act 2009 to amend the law to enable its powers under the Act to be used effectively may, by section 75(3), be exercised retrospectively where the Treasury considers this 'necessary or desirable'.

Additionally, the language of a statute, although not expressly stating that it is retrospective, may make it clear that it is, as in legislation legalising acts that were illegal when done or freeing those to whom the statute applies from liability. The Indemnity Act 1920 gave the government and those holding public office a general indemnity in respect of acts done in good faith for the defence of the realm or otherwise in the public interest during World War 1. Legislation may also retrospectively expose individuals to liability. The War Crimes Act 1991 gave UK courts the jurisdiction to try homicides committed in German occupied territory during World War II that were war crimes and were allegedly committed by people who later became British citizens or residents.

Where legislation does not expressly or by necessary implication address the question of retroactivity, two questions arise: whether the presumption applies and, if so, whether it has been rebutted. What Lord Rodger in *Wilson v First County Trust Ltd* described (at [212]) as 'the powerful presumption against retroactivity' meant that section 3 of the HRA 1998 did not apply to the rights and obligations arising under a loan made before the HRA came into force. Accordingly, the lender could not invoke the right under Article 1 of the First Protocol to the ECHR not to be deprived of its contractual rights to remove the borrower's statutory protection under the Consumer Protection Act 1974. This was so although the strong interpretative obligation in section 3 'so far as possible' to read and give effect to legislation in a way which is compatible with ECHR rights applies to legislation whenever enacted. The presumption was fortified by the fact that section 22(4), providing a defence to proceedings brought by a public authority based on an ECHR right 'whenever the act in question took place', showed that where Parliament wished to provide retroactive effect in the HRA it did so expressly.

Not all statutes which affect past events and transactions fall within the presumption. It does not apply to matters of pure procedure or to statutes which make, as they often do, prospective changes which alter previous rights and liabilities but do so only for the future. Moreover, if a statute does not affect rights previously enjoyed as of a time prior to the amending, there is no problem of retroactivity, and thus no problem with this aspect of the rule of law. Accordingly, a statute removing a right to deduct certain expenses when computing income for tax purposes which did not affect deductions made before it came into force is not subject to the presumption: *Gustavson Drilling (1964) Ltd v Minister of National Revenue* [1977] 1 SCR 271, 279–80 *per* Dickson J (Supreme Court of Canada). Again, an order under section 28 of the Criminal Justice and Court Services Act 2000 disqualifying a defendant from working with children in the future did not offend against the presumption or the rule of law where the offending behaviour had occurred before section 28 came into force: *R v Field* [2003] 1 WLR 882. The new legislation applied immediately to the future effects of a situation which arose under the old legislation.

With the exception of fundamental rights which are considered so important that they are 'non-derogable', that is cannot be limited or suspended, such as not to be subjected to torture or inhuman or degrading treatment contrary to ECHR Article 3, no one has a right to continuance of the law as it stood in the past. Other fundamental rights, such as those under the ECHR, and rights characterised as 'vested' rights (sometimes by 'essentially circular' reasoning) are, however, subject to a presumption against even prospective interference unless this is done unambiguously: *Wilson v First County Trust per* Lord Rodger at [196]. In the case of fundamental rights, any interference must also be in accordance with the principles of legality and proportionality: see chapters five and nine.

Where the presumption against retrospectivity applies, there are many judicial statements about its strength, particularly about legislation creating new crimes or liabilities to tax. But there are also many examples of judicial willingness to conclude that the presumption has been rebutted. This is one reason that in *Wilson v First County Trust* Lord Nicholls at [19] stated that the presumption against retrospectivity is 'vague and

imprecise'. It has also often been said that the underlying rationale of the
presumption and the circumstances in which it will be rebutted is 'simple
fairness' and that 'the greater the unfairness, the more it is to be expected
that Parliament will make that clear if that is intended': see for example
Lord Mustill in *L'Office Cherifien des Phosphates v Yamashita-Shinnihon
Steamship Co* [1994] 1 AC 486, 525A. Fairness is not assessed by considering the merits of the particular case, but (see 528C) 'the generality
of the rights which Parliament must have contemplated would suffer'
if a provision took effect retrospectively. In the absence of reasons for
regarding a particular result as fair or unfair, however, a conclusory term
such as 'fairness' does not explain either the applicability of the presumption against retroactivity or its rebuttal: see Juratowitch especially at 224.
What, therefore, are the factors in play?

The presumption is likely to be more difficult to rebut where retroactivity would affect many past transactions or personal liberty, for
instance where legislation increases the punishment for prior criminal
conduct. So, in *Re Baretto* [1994] QB 392 and *McCool* [2018] UKSC 23
statutory changes to the criminal confiscation scheme did not apply to
confiscation orders made or offences committed before the changes came
into force.

The presumption is likely to be easier to rebut where the court considers that certainty will not be affected by retroactivity, where this is
necessary to protect fundamental human rights, or in respect of conduct regarded as heinous. It will also be easier where a statute abolishes
an anachronistic rule based on a legal fiction, such as the abolition of
the liability of a husband for the tort of his wife by the Law Reform
(Married Women and Tortfeasors) Act 1935: see *Barber v Pigdon* [1937]
1 KB 664, at 677 *per* Scott LJ. A court may also be more willing to conclude that the presumption has been rebutted where the legislation is
directed against tax evasion or to prevent tax savings that are considered
unmerited. *Re John Mander Pension Trustees* [2015] UKSC 56 concerned
whether withdrawal of approval for a pension scheme took effect from
the date when notice was given to the taxpayer or from the date specified
by the tax authorities, some four years before the notice. A bare majority
of the Supreme Court concluded that the withdrawal of approval took
effect from the date specified although that meant the statute operated
retroactively. Lord Reed stated at [52] that 'securing the restoration of
the taxpayer's benefit from unmerited tax savings does not in substance

involve the imposition of retrospective taxation, but rather the recovery of tax which was foregone at an earlier date'. The minority considered that, absent clear words, this retroactivity which in principle gave rise to liability for substantial sums in interest during a period when the taxpayer believed the scheme was approved was not justified.

## IV. REASONABLE STABILITY

From a rule of law perspective, it is important for the law to be kept up to date. But frequency of change may itself be a driver of complexity and an impediment to accessibility because of the difficulty of keeping up with the changes and ascertaining the current position. The frequent changes to the regulations made imposing restrictions to deal with the COVID 19 pandemic, and the gap between what is announced and the actual content of the regulations, which are often published later, have vividly demonstrated this. It has been estimated that lockdown rules were changed over 60 times in the first nine months of the pandemic. But, while government must be entitled to react swiftly to emergencies, frequency of change is not a problem confined to emergencies.

In *R (Noone) v Governor of HMP Drake Hall* [2010] UKSC 30 at [80] Lord Judge observed that 'for too many years now the administration of criminal justice has been engulfed by a relentless tidal wave of legislation. The tide is always in flow: it has never ebbed'. Spencer 2008, 586 estimated that in the decade after 1997 57 Acts of Parliament altered the rules of criminal justice.

The frequency of changes to the Immigration Rules has also attracted criticism by the courts and the Law Commission 2020, §4.11 and §1.17. In 2013 there were 12 sets of changes, although there has been some reduction since. In *Hossain v Home Secretary* [2015] EWCA Civ 207 the Court of Appeal stated at [30] that

> [t]he detail, the number of documents that have to be consulted, the number of changes in rules and policy guidance, and the difficulty advisers face in ascertaining which previous version of the rule or guidance applies and obtaining it are real obstacles to achieving predictable consistency and restoring public trust in the system, particularly in an area of law that lay people and people whose first language is not English need to understand.

# V. OPEN JUSTICE

The need for law to be accessible in the ways discussed is linked to the principle of open justice. That principle requires that hearings in courts and tribunals should generally be in public, with advance notice of the cases, and with decisions publicly available. It is fundamentally important to protect litigants from the administration of justice in secret with no public scrutiny. This 'is not a mere procedural rule' but 'a fundamental common law principle' (*Al Rawi v Security Service* [2011] UKSC 34 at [11]) and a 'constitutional principle': *R (Guardian News) and Media v Westminster Magistrates Court* [2012] EWCA Civ 420 at [69].

Open justice ultimately supports the rule of law by enabling the public through the media to see that justice is being done in a particular case by scrutinising the judicial process and the conduct of the parties and others involved in litigation. It has been said to be the best means for achieving the confidence and respect of the public: *Scott v Scott* [1913] AC 417, 463 and *R (Binyam Mohamed) v Foreign Secretary* [2010] EWCA Civ 65 at [38]–[39]. It thus represents an element of democratic accountability even where the manner of media reporting is insensitive and unbalanced: *Guardian News & Media v HM Treasury* [2010] UKSC 1 at [63]–[65].

Over the past 16 years the principle has led to the increasing use of cameras in the senior courts and the livestreaming of some civil cases and, since 2020, sentencing remarks in some criminal cases. It is forbidden to film defendants, victims, witnesses, lawyers and court staff. The need for justice to be seen to be done must be balanced against the need to avoid outside influences and sensationalism influencing proceedings. Susskind 2020 196 acknowledges that the introduction of online courts where only the parties are 'present' has an impact on this principle. But he considers that if online courts can deliver just results in low value disputes by a fair procedure there is a compelling case 'to give some ground on open justice'.

The position differs for administrative decision-making by government and regulatory bodies. While some formal administrative procedures dealing with proposals for major infrastructure projects such as motorways or airports are in public, most administrative decision-making is not. It is, however, subject to rules to ensure procedural fairness, and challenges by appeals and judicial reviews will be in public.

Exceptions to open justice in courts and tribunals must be justified, and they are in certain cases. As a result of press campaigns against 'secret justice' in family courts, the tensions between open justice and legitimate expectations of privacy and confidentiality for the family are perhaps the best known. There is particular controversy about departing from the principle in family cases concerning financial arrangements after relationship breakdowns: *Norman v Norman* [2017] EWCA Civ 49. The case for such departure is stronger in cases concerning children or mentally incapacitated patients, whose best interests are a primary consideration for the court and where important issues of privacy are engaged. But in cases in which the outcome may be serious, such as interference by the state with family life or liberty by separating parents and their children, or by compulsorily detaining a mentally incapacitated person, account also has to be taken of the public interest in knowing how the coercive power of the state is exercised.

There are other circumstances in which a private or closed hearing and limited or no reporting may be necessary in the interests of justice or in the public interest. They include cases where publicity would defeat the object of the hearing, as in applications for a search order or a freezing injunction to restrain a person from dealing with any assets, where commercially valuable secret information is in issue, and cases involving national security.

In a private hearing the departure from open justice only affects the wider public because the litigants participate fully in the process and receive the judgment: *Bank Mellat v HM Treasury (No 1)* [2013] UKSC 38 at [3]. More fundamental problems for rule of law values and the principle of natural justice arise where one party wants the decision-maker to rely on material not disclosed to the other party. Those, and the way our law has sought to protect that party, in particular by the use of 'special advocates', are discussed at 93–95.

# 5

## Avoiding Arbitrariness

This chapter considers how the principle of the rule of law prevents arbitrariness. It deals with certainty and flexibility, uncertain and ill-defined laws, the constraints on the exercise of statutory and prerogative discretion by public authorities to prevent arbitrariness, and the power of government ministers to amend or repeal primary legislation using delegated legislation, pursuant to what are called Henry VIII clauses, and thus to shift power from the legislature to the executive.

The principle of legal certainty at the heart of the rule of law means that legal provisions which interfere with individual rights must be formulated with sufficient precision to enable citizens to regulate their conduct and to be able to foresee the consequences of a given action. In *Sunday Times v UK* (1979) 2 EHRR 245 at [49] it was stated that:

> Those consequences need not be foreseeable with absolute certainty: experience shows this to be unattainable. Again, whilst certainty is highly desirable, it may bring in its train excessive rigidity and the law must be able to keep pace with changing circumstances. Accordingly, many laws are inevitably couched in terms which, to a greater or lesser extent, are vague and whose interpretation and application are questions of practice.

The common law origins of the principle of legal certainty, also reflected in what is known as the principle of legality, are thus complemented and enhanced by the requirements of the ECHR.

## I. CERTAINTY AND FLEXIBILITY

Although Hobbes in *Leviathan* rejected the view that the law binds the ultimate sovereign, he had earlier recognised in *de Cive* that to shape behaviour effectively and promote clarity and stability, those in power need rules that are clear, general and prospective. This is because, in order to shape behaviour, those who are governed need to be able to predict what will happen to them if they embark on a course of action, such as driving through a red traffic light or lighting a bonfire in their garden.

Certainty is undoubtedly important, despite the degree of rigidity and formalism that is often a necessary price for the increased certainty that can be obtained from clear, accessible rules. But absolute certainty is unattainable, and the achievement of reasonable certainty can be difficult. First, as Plato observed, the rule of law is a problematic concept because 'people and situations differ, and human affairs are characterised by an almost permanent state of instability': *The Statesman*, 294b. For him and other rule-sceptics, 'bright line' and general rules which operate in a binary way and are justified as promoting certainty and predictability may overlook this. They argue that ignoring such differences deflects attention from the underlying purpose served by the rule in question. Moreover, as seen at 33–35, all texts leave some choice as to how, at the margin, they are to be interpreted.

The degree of uncertainty and vagueness resulting from the breadth and open textured nature of the rule of law principle itself has been mentioned at 2 and 19–20. Moreover, the degree to which discretion is needed by officials in a modern complex state means that statutes (primary legislation) often provide only a broad framework not suited to determining the outcome in a particular fact situation, or at least not suited to doing so consistently. They deal with this by empowering officials to make more detailed rules (delegated legislation) or guidelines in respect of such decision-making. Such rules or guidelines may be less accessible and be more complex because of frequent changes made to address developments in policy or to rectify errors revealed by decisions of courts and tribunals. Those features tend to lead to less legal certainty and transparency and to an increased risk of mistakes by citizens, officials and even by courts and tribunals. Notable examples of this, discussed at 49, are the Immigration Rules and Coronavirus Regulations which have been changed frequently and without adequate accountability or scrutiny.

Both over-reliance on rules (formalism) and undue scepticism about the value of rules are open to criticism. All legal systems involve a compromise between the need for certain rules and the need to respond to factual and evaluative differences. Professor HLA Hart, 126–27, stated that if such differences are ignored, or insufficiently recognised, and the need for the exercise of choice in the application of general rules to particular cases is disguised or minimised, a measure of certainty or predictability is secured 'at the cost of blindly prejudging what is to be done in a range of future cases, about whose composition we are ignorant'. For Hart, the effect of such over-reliance on rules was to

> succeed in settling in advance, but also in the dark, issues which can only reasonably be settled when they arise and are identified. ... The rigidity of our classifications will thus war with our aims in having or maintaining the rule.

The problems created by over-broad rules can be illustrated by the legislation making it an absolute offence for any driver, including the drivers of fire engines and ambulances, to fail to stop at a red traffic light. *Buckoke v Greater London Council* [1971] Ch 655 concerned the lawfulness of a direction by the chief officer of a fire brigade that drivers of fire engines were subject to the general law of the land but recognised that drivers might decide to commit technical offences by driving through a red light. A driver who wished to do this was directed to stop at the red light and only to proceed after being reasonably satisfied that the road was clear and there was no risk of collision. The Court of Appeal affirmed that the legislation meant that drivers committed an offence even where they took those steps. There was no defence of necessity. The absolute or 'bright line' rule in the legislation deflected attention from its undoubted purpose of promoting road safety. It fastened on a feature present in an ordinary case, here going through a red light, and insisted that this was both necessary and sufficient for there to be an offence, even where it penalised the driver of an emergency vehicle who had acted with all prudence and without risk to others.

In *Buckoke's* case the Court recognised the need for a more nuanced approach. It stated that the rigour of the law was mitigated because of the practice of paying any fines imposed on drivers out of public funds. It stated that it would be further mitigated by the police not prosecuting a driver who stopped and only proceeded after seeing that the road was clear. These two mitigations enabled it to find that the chief fire officer's direction was lawful. But the court also stated that Parliament should change the law to exempt drivers of public service vehicles when for dealing with emergencies.

## II. UNCERTAIN AND ILL-DEFINED LAWS

The overriding nature of Parliamentary sovereignty means that the principle of legal certainty cannot apply directly to primary legislation.

Uncertainty resulting from the use of general words or ambiguity is, however, likely to be resolved by giving a restrictive interpretation to a statute which interferes with fundamental rights or imposes a criminal penalty. This approach is reflected by the principle of legality and the presumption against retroactive legislation considered in chapter four. So, the common law crime of causing a public nuisance is sufficiently certain provided it is confined to well-established situations where the defendant's act harmed a section of the public, the community, rather than simply harming individuals: *Rimmington* [2005] UKHL 63 at [36]–[38] and [47]. But where the vagueness of a law which purports to create criminal liability makes it impossible to identify the conduct which is prohibited and a court is forced to guess at the ingredients of a purported crime, any conviction for it would be unsafe: *Misra and Srivastava* [2004] EWCA Crim 2375 at [34]. Similarly, a statute prohibiting civil servants from expressing opinions on 'politically controversial matters' was an insufficiently clear restriction of the right under the constitution of Antigua and Barbuda to freedom of expression, even if read down to apply only when prohibition was reasonably required for proper performance of official functions. This was because leaving it to individual civil servants to decide whether or not they are not complying with the rule without guidance was insufficiently precise: *De Freitas v Permanent Secretary of Ministry of Agriculture* [1999] 1 AC 69, 78.

Where the meaning of delegated legislation cannot be ascertained with a reasonable degree of certainty, it will be held to be outside the power conferred by primary legislation and void. The cases, however, show that a person who contends that such legislation is insufficiently clear to satisfy common law requirements of certainty must overcome a high hurdle: *R (Gul) v Justice Secretary* [2014] EWHC 373 (Admin) at [58] and *McEldowney v Forde* [1971] AC 632, 665. For example, while the identification in a by-law of a prohibited military area by a thick black line on a small-scale map was not clear, the by-law was not invalid at common law. Although a person near the boundary would not be certain whether he was in the prohibited area, it was said that there will always be a borderline of uncertainty and that a provision would only be invalid if it was so uncertain in its language as to have no ascertainable meaning or be so unclear in its effect as to be incapable of certain application in any case: *Percy v Hall* [1997] QB 924. But by-laws providing that 'no person shall wilfully annoy passengers in the streets' and prohibiting flying hang-gliders over a pleasure ground without specifying the height below which the offence was committed were held to be invalid: *Nash v Findlay* (1901) 85 LT 682 and *Staden v Tarjani* (1980) 78 LGR 614.

# III. CONSTRAINTS ON DISCRETION

In systems based on the rule of law such as the common law and the ECHR with its requirement of 'lawfulness', '[t]he public must not be vulnerable to interference by public officials acting on any personal whim, caprice, malice, predilection or purpose other than that for which the power was conferred': *R (Gillan) v Metropolitan Police Commissioner* [2006] UKHL 12 at [34]. Lord Bingham explained that 'this is what, in this context, is meant by arbitrariness, which is the antithesis of legality'. It follows that 'unfettered governmental discretion is a contradiction in terms': *R v Tower Hamlets LBC, ex p Chetnik Developments Ltd* [1988] AC 858, 872.

There are two elements to this aspect of the rule of law. One is the need to indicate the scope of a discretionary power with sufficient clarity, particularly in relation to discretion to interfere with a right under the ECHR. The other, which I consider first, is how courts should give effect to the rule of law's need to avoid arbitrariness and arbitrary distinctions without taking over a function that Parliament has given to a government minister, local authority or regulatory body.

It is the function of the courts to determine questions of law and to ensure that public officials do not extend the area over which the legislature has granted them jurisdiction. Accordingly, the holder of a discretionary power must correctly understand the law that regulates the decision-making power and must give effect to it. If an error of law is made, the decision can be judicially reviewed on the ground of 'illegality' and is a nullity. In respect of errors of law, jurisdictional questions and absolute rights such as the rights to life and not to be subjected to torture or inhuman treatment set out in ECHR Articles 2 and 3, the decision-maker has no leeway. In other cases, including those involving qualified rights such as those set out in ECHR Articles 8–11, on which see 150, the role of the court is supervisory. The control exercised by the supervisory jurisdiction recognises that 'the very concept of … discretion involves a right to choose between more than one possible course of action upon which there is room for reasonable people to hold differing opinions as to which is to be preferred': *Secretary of State for Education and Science v Tameside MBC* [1977] AC 1014, 1064.

The techniques of control developed over the last 100 years recognise that it is not for courts to substitute their choice for that of the body which has been given the power by Parliament, or which holds it under the prerogative. With two exceptions, they seek to respect that body's power of choice by focussing primarily on the decision-making process. The courts will consider whether the process adhered to certain standards rather than considering the merits of the decision itself. Discretionary powers must be used to promote the policy and objects of the legislation which confer them. Decision-makers are also limited by principles of propriety of purpose and relevance, principles which are intimately related to each other and to 'illegality' as a ground for judicial review.

A power must not be used for a purpose other than that for which it was conferred. Where there are mixed purposes, the question is whether the dominant purposes are lawful. For example, the Home Secretary was not permitted to use a statutory power to revoke television licences in order to raise money by revoking the licences of a large number of people who had bought a new licence early in order to avoid a prospectively announced price increase: *Congreve v Home Office* [1976] QB 629. It has been stated that the principle of propriety of purpose 'is one of the most important bulwarks which our predecessors so painstakingly erected against arbitrary acts of the executive': *R (GC) v Metropolitan Police Commissioner* [2011] UKSC 21 at [107] *per* Lord Rodger.

There is a link between propriety of purpose and the requirement of relevance which means that a decision-maker must take into account matters legally relevant to the exercise of a statutory power and not take into account irrelevant matters. In *Padfield v Minister of Agriculture, Fisheries and Food* [1968] AC 997, for example, a minister was not entitled to refuse to refer milk producers' complaints to a statutory committee on the ground that, if the committee upheld the complaints, he might find himself in an embarrassing situation because he would be expected to act. That was both an improper purpose and an irrelevant consideration.

The two exceptions to the focus on the decision-making process rather than the merits of the decision itself are the substantive grounds of *Wednesbury* unreasonableness or irrationality, formulated in *Associated Picture Houses Ltd. v Wednesbury Corporation* [1948] 1 KB 223, and the principle of proportionality. The origins of proportionality lie in German administrative law, from where it moved via the Strasbourg court to Canada and a number of other common law jurisdictions: *Bank Mellat v HM Treasury (No 2)* [2013] UKSC 39 at [68]–[76] on which see 67 and 154–55. Significant aspects of proportionality have been incorporated into domestic common law, particularly where the discretionary power affects fundamental rights: see *Pham v Home Secretary* [2015] UKSC 19 at [106]–[107] and [117]–[119], on deprivation of UK citizenship, and *Kennedy v Charity Commissioner* [2014] UKSC 20 at [54] on a refusal to disclose information of genuine public interest requested for journalistic purposes.

Both rationality and proportionality involve considerations of weight and balance which also respect the decision-making body's power of choice. But in *R (Keyu) v Foreign Secretary* [2015] UKSC 69 at [131]–[132] Lord Neuberger stated that the implications of a shift from rationality to proportionality would be 'profound in constitutional terms' because 'it would require the courts to consider the balance which the decision-maker has struck between competing interests (often a public interest against a private interest) and the weight to be accorded to each such interest'. Lord Kerr at [252], however, questioned the constitutional importance of the change and the extent of the implications. Whether or not proportionality is now a general ground of review at common law, *Kennedy* and *Pham* demonstrate that it has undoubtedly altered rationality review, particularly in the context of fundamental rights: Beatson and Foubister, 93–95.

In the case of rationality, significant choice is left as a result of the high threshold required by the basic test: is the decision so absurd that no sensible person could consider that it in fact lay within the power ostensibly conferred? The classic example is the dismissal of a teacher because she had red hair. But the concept also includes decisions lacking in any logical basis or affected by flawed logic: see *R v N & E Devon HA, ex p Coughlan* [2001] QB 213 at [65], discussed at 62–3. It also supports more intense scrutiny of decisions affecting fundamental rights or important interests. They must be justified by an important public interest, and the more substantial the interference with such rights, the more the court will require by way of justification.

Proportionality requires there to be a proper balance between the adverse effects of a decision on rights, liberties or interests and the purpose of a discretionary power. United Kingdom jurisdictions assess this with a structured four-stage test. They ask whether: (i) the objective is sufficiently important to justify the limitation of a fundamental right, (ii) the limitation is rationally connected to the objective, (iii) a less intrusive limitation could have been used, and (iv) having regard to (ii) and (iii), the limitation strikes a fair balance between the rights of the individual and the interests of the community: *R (Tigere) v Secretary of State for Business, Innovation and Skills* [2015] UKSC 57 at [33].

As to the standards needed to indicate the scope of a discretionary power with sufficient clarity, one is to recognise that it is a fundamental principle of justice that like cases be treated alike. It follows that in similar cases discretion to make rules and to apply those rules should be exercised in a similar way. For example, in *R (Middlebrook Mushrooms Ltd) v Agricultural Wages Board* [2004] EWHC (Admin) 1635 at [74] the exclusion of mushroom growers from delegated legislation providing a reduced minimum wage for harvesters was held to be *Wednesbury* unreasonable and unlawful because it did not observe the 'cardinal principle of public administration that all persons in a similar position should be treated similarly'. A broad discretion without standards may also mask unlawful discrimination, such as where Immigration Officers routinely treated Roma applicants for leave to enter the UK with longer and more intrusive questioning than non-Roma: *R v Immigration Officer, Prague Airport, ex p European Roma Rights Centre* [2004] UKHL 55, and see the criticism of exercises of discretion exclusively on 'hunch' in the discussion of the *Gillan* case at 65.

In *R (Gallagher Group) v Competition and Markets Authority* [2018] UKSC 25, however, the Supreme Court considered that the relevant principles are rationality and legitimate expectation. The court stated that a requirement of consistency and equal treatment is not a distinct principle of administrative law and, see [24] and [50], would 'multiply categories' and 'undermine the coherence of the law'. *Gallagher* concerned financial penalties imposed on eight tobacco companies for price fixing. Six of the companies successfully appealed. One of the two which did not had sought and was given an assurance that it would be treated in the same way as the companies which appealed but the other neither knew of this nor sought an assurance. The court held that there was no entitlement to be given an assurance, it was not irrational to treat the two non-appellants differently and, (see [63]), the fact of the assurance was 'a powerful objective justification for unequal treatment'. Although, as Lord Scarman stated in *HTV v Price Commission* [1976] ICR 170, 192, inconsistency is not necessarily unfair, it is unfortunate that the court did not consider its important decision in *Mandalia v Home Secretary* [2015] UKSC 59 at [29] which approved the statement by Laws LJ in *R (Nadarajah) v Home Secretary* [2005] EWCA Civ 1363 at [68] that there is a broad 'requirement of good administration, by which public bodies ought to deal straightforwardly and consistently with the public'.

There are a number of ways in which courts seek to achieve the measure of certainty and foreseeability required by the rule of law without the rigid rules which completely exclude discretion. They are all aspects of the principle of consistency.

The first is by enabling an administrative body to have broad rules and policies which are in line with the policy and purpose of the statutory or common law power conferring the discretion. Examples include whether to prosecute in assisted suicide cases and immigration practice referred to at 15–16. Such rules and policies 'are an essential element in securing the coherent and consistent performance of administrative functions' and 'provided that the policy is not regarded as binding and the authority still retains a free exercise of discretion the policy may serve the useful purpose of giving reasonable guidance both to applicants and decision-makers': *R (Alconbury Development Ltd) v Secretary of State for the Environment* [2001] UKHL 23 at [143]. Using them has always been possible provided that the discretion is exercised in each case and the decision-maker has not 'fettered' its discretion by overcommitting itself to a particular decision or approach without leaving space for an exceptional or unanticipated case.

In *British Oxygen Co Ltd v Minister of Technology* [1971] AC 610, 625 a policy stating that a discretionary power to make a grant towards capital expenditure on machinery or plant would not be exercised in respect of items costing less than £25 was not invalid where the minister carefully considered all that the company said in support of its application for a grant in respect of gas cylinders of a total value of £4 million but costing under £20 each. But in *R v Home Secretary, ex p Venables* [1998] AC 407, 496–97 a broad discretion to review the 'tariff period' of an indeterminate sentence of detention during Her Majesty's pleasure of a 10-year old convicted of a notorious murder was unlawfully fettered by the inflexibility of a policy. The policy only permitted review on grounds relating to the circumstances of the crime and the offender's state of mind at that time and ruled out of consideration other factors such as the young offender's welfare, development and progress as he got older. Additionally, too rigid a policy about non-prosecution of difficult and ethically sensitive cases such as those on assisted suicide might breach Article 1 of the Bill of Rights 1689 which provides that the 'pretended power of suspending ... the execution of laws' without the consent of Parliament 'is illegal'.

The influence of the common law requirement of 'legality' and the ECHR's principle of certainty means that such rules and policies are now positively encouraged and required as safeguards against arbitrariness. For example, a hospital's published seclusion policy sufficed to make a discretionary power to detain a mental patient in seclusion lawful even though it departed from the Secretary of State's statutory Code of Conduct: *R (Munjaz) v Mersey Care NHS Trust* [2005] UKHL 58 at [34]. As Parliament had deliberately made provision for a non-binding Code, there was no obligation on hospitals to have a seclusion policy that conformed in every respect to it. In *R (Lumba) v Home Secretary* [2011] UKSC 12 at [34] Lord Dyson stated:

> The rule of law calls for a transparent statement by the executive of the circumstances in which the broad statutory criteria will be exercised. Just as arrest and surveillance powers need to be transparently identified through codes of practice and immigration powers need to be transparently identified through the immigration rules, so too the immigration detention powers need to be transparently identified through formulated policy statements.

While such policies are encouraged, it must not be forgotten that administrative policies may change with changing circumstances, including changes in the political complexion of governments and 'the liberty to make such changes is something that is inherent in our constitutional form of government': *Hughes v DHSS* [1985] AC 776 at 788.

A second way in which courts seek to achieve the measure of certainty required by the rule of law is the protection given to legitimate expectations that have arisen where a decision-maker has, by a representation or a regular practice, led someone to believe he or she will receive or retain a benefit. The expectation may be procedural or substantive. For instance there was a procedural expectation to be consulted before a decision was made in *Council of Civil Service Unions v Minister for the Civil Service* [1985] AC 374, the '*GCHQ* case' on which see 68. By contrast there was a substantive expectation in *R v N & E Devon HA, ex p Coughlan* [2001] QB 213, where a resident of a NHS care home was led to understand that she had 'a home for life' but the Health Authority later decided to close the home because it had become 'a prohibitively expensive white elephant'. In such cases, the public authority may be entitled to change its policy but only if there are overriding reasons for departing from the expectation raised. In *Coughlan*'s case there were no such reasons because the health authority did not offer the resident an equivalent facility and failed to weigh the competing interests correctly.

Notwithstanding the availability of these purely common law techniques to prevent arbitrariness and promote reasonable certainty and consistency, there are a number of notable cases in which discretionary powers upheld by English courts have been found by the Strasbourg court not to satisfy the requirement of lawfulness. In these cases, the powers did not indicate with sufficient clarity the scope of the discretion to interfere with a right set out in the ECHR or otherwise lacked the precision required. The examples below show that in such cases Parliament almost invariably seeks to provide structure and certainty by legislation.

The first example concerns telephone tapping. Its implicit statutory recognition in the Post Office Act 1969 if authorised by a warrant of the Home Secretary was held to be lawful in *Malone v Metropolitan Police Commissioner (No 2)* [1979] Ch 344. The court, following Dicey and ignoring the special position of government officials, considered England not to be 'a country where everything is forbidden except what is expressly permitted: it is a country where everything is permitted except what is expressly forbidden'. But in *Malone v UK* (1984) 7 EHRR 14 at [67]–[68] the Strasbourg Court, while recognising that some secret surveillance is in exceptional circumstances necessary in a democratic society to counter threats of subversion and terrorism, held that 'it would be contrary to the rule of law for the legal discretion granted to the executive to be expressed in terms of an unfettered power'. The discretion must be expressed with sufficient clarity to give the individual adequate protection against arbitrary interference. Soon afterwards the interception of communications was put on a statutory footing by the Interception of Communications Act 1985. It is now governed by the Regulation of Investigatory Powers Act 2000.

What happened in relation to DNA samples and profiles and fingerprints taken in connection with the investigation of an offence was similar. The retention of the samples of unconvicted persons, save in exceptional circumstances, was held to be lawful by the House of Lords in *R v Chief Constable of South Yorkshire, ex p S & Marper* [2004] UKHL 39 because any infringement of the right to respect for private life set out in ECHR Article 8 was modest and was justified by the need to detect serious crime. The Strasbourg Court differed. It regarded the position as similar to that for telephone tapping, secret surveillance and covert intelligence gathering. It did not consider that the rather general terms of the statute that retained samples must not be used by any person except for purposes related to the prevention or detection of crime, the investigation of an offence, or the conduct of a prosecution, were in accordance with the law. It was

> essential in this context ... to have clear, detailed rules governing the scope and application of measures, as well as minimum safeguards concerning, *inter alia*, duration, storage, usage, access of third parties, procedures for preserving the integrity and confidentiality of data and procedures for its destruction, thus providing sufficient guarantees against the risk of abuse and arbitrariness: *S & Marper v UK* (2008) 48 EHRR 50 at [99].

Parliament addressed the matter in the Crime and Security Act 2010, and it is now regulated by the Protection of Freedoms Act 2012.

The third example concerns the common law concept of breach of the peace and the power to bind over. Both are deeply rooted in the English legal system. The first dates back to the tenth century. The statutory origin of binding over is the Justices of the Peace Act 1361. The power to bind over is often used to deal with protesters and thus involves possible breaches of the freedoms of expression and assembly set out in ECHR Articles 10 and 11. If used to bind over only those who have committed breaches of the peace it meets the requirement of legal certainty because that concept has been clarified by English courts since 1948. It is now clear that a breach of the peace is only established where an individual causes harm to persons or property or appears likely to do so, or acts in a manner the natural consequence of which would provoke others to commit violence: *Steel v UK* (1998) 28 EHRR 39 at [55]–[56], about a protest against a grouse shoot. But, as Law Commission 1994 §4.34 anticipated, where conduct did not and was not likely to occasion a breach of the peace, the position differs. *Hashman & Harrup v UK* (2000) 30 EHRR 241 held that binding over protesters at a hunt who were blowing a hunting horn and making noise, requiring them not to act *contra bonos mores*, that is to be of 'good behaviour', did not satisfy the requirement of legality. This was because conduct *contra bonos mores* is defined as behaviour which is 'wrong rather than right in the judgment of the majority of contemporary fellow citizens', and that did not describe the conduct itself or provide sufficient indication of the conduct to be avoided to be safe from sanction.

The fourth example concerns statutory power to stop and search a person even where there is no reasonable suspicion that person has committed an offence or is about to. Section 44 of the Terrorism Act 2000 empowered this where it was authorised by a senior police officer who considered it 'expedient' for the prevention of acts of terrorism and confirmed by the Secretary of State. Its lawfulness was challenged in *R (Gillan) v Commissioner of Metropolitan Police* by protesters at an arms fair who did not know that they were liable to be stopped and searched without reasonable suspicion. The House of Lords held that the section satisfied the requirement of lawfulness because the authorisation and exercise of the powers were defined and limited with considerable precision, even though neither the 2000 Act nor Code A of the Police and Criminal Evidence Act 1984 required the fact or the details of any authorisation to be published in any way, even retrospectively: see [2006] UKHL 12 [14] and [34]–[35].

As it had in other cases, the Strasbourg Court recognised that domestic legislation cannot provide for every eventuality and that the level of precision depends to a considerable degree on the content and context of the legislative instrument. But it concluded that there was a clear risk of arbitrariness in the grant of such a broad discretion to police officers. The decision to exercise the power was based exclusively on the 'hunch' or 'professional intuition' of the officer concerned. It was unnecessary for the officer to demonstrate the existence of any reasonable suspicion, or even subjectively to suspect anything about the person stopped and searched: *Gillan & Quinton v UK* (2010) 50 EHRR 45 at [83] and [85]. Again, Parliament addressed the matter by amendments to the 2000 Act in sections 59 and 61 of the Protection of Freedoms Act 2012.

This difference between the approach of our domestic courts and the Strasbourg Court in part reflects the common law at that stage not recognising the importance of the individual interest affected; privacy in *Malone* and *S & Marper*; a prior restraint on freedom of expression in *Hashman & Harrup*; and freedom of assembly in *Gillan*. In part it reflects inconsistency in giving full effect to the principle of legality when considering whether to read down general words in the way referred to at 34, 123 and 141. But in the case of other interests affected, such as the rights to liberty and to property, and other rights recognised to be fundamental or constitutional, the common law has imposed requirements to enhance foreseeability and predictability and thus to avoid arbitrariness. The approach taken in cases such as *Entick v Carrington* (1765) 19 St Trials 1029 at 1066, on which see 140, where Lord Camden CJ stated that 'property is preserved sacred and incommunicable' except where it is abridged by Parliament is one example. *De Freitas*'s case, referred to at 56, is another.

In the context of the clarity required about the scope of a discretion, a good example is the approach to the right to liberty developed in cases of immigration detention pursuant to paragraph 16 of Schedule 2 to the Immigration Act 1971. That provision contains a very broadly worded discretionary power to detain those who require leave to enter or remain in the United Kingdom, including those who have applied for asylum. It authorises detention pending examination by an immigration officer, and pending decisions to give or refuse leave to enter, to direct removal and to remove pursuant to such directions. In a line of cases since 1984, culminating in the decision of the Supreme Court in *R (Lumba) v Secretary of State for the Home Department* [2011] UKSC 12, referred to at 62, the common law has developed principles governing this power to save it from what was described by Laws LJ as the vice of arbitrariness: *R (SK (Zimbabwe) v Home Secretary* [2008] EWCA Civ 1204 at [33]. The detention must be for the statutory purposes of making or implementing a deportation order alone and cannot continue for longer than a period which is reasonable in all the circumstances. As to how long is reasonable, decisions of the courts have held that an exhaustive list of relevant circumstances is neither possible nor desirable. But they include the obstacles to deportation, the Home Secretary's diligence in seeking to surmount those obstacles, the conditions of detention, the health of the detainee, and the risk of the detainee absconding or committing criminal offences if released: *Lumba* at [104]–[105].

In determining the degree of clarity and level of precision that will be required and the intensity of scrutiny of a discretionary power, as observed at 36 and 65, context is important. In certain contexts, the courts are likely to exercise restraint because the issue is one which they are less well equipped to determine. For example, it may concern what the general interest requires as a matter of policy, which in a democracy are 'decisions made by democratically elected bodies or persons accountable to them' even if the application of that policy to determine the liability of a particular person is then a matter for independent and impartial courts and tribunals: *R (Alconbury Development Ltd) v Secretary of State for the Environment* [2001] UKHL 23 at [69].

In *Nottinghamshire CC v Secretary of State for the Environment* [1986] AC 240 it was said that while some matters of public financial administration would raise a justiciable issue as to the true construction of a statute, it was not constitutionally appropriate save in exceptional circumstances to quash central government guidance to local authorities on expenditure which had been approved by the House of Commons. That was a matter of political judgement for the minister and Parliament.

Other areas in which restraint is often shown are prosecutorial discretion, international relations, the making of treaties, macro-economic policy, the allocation of scarce resources, and national security. But even in such areas the exercise of a discretionary power may be set aside. So, notwithstanding national security concerns, in *A v Home Secretary* [2004] UKHL 56 ('the Belmarsh case') the indefinite detention without trial of foreign terrorist suspects was held not to be strictly required and not to be 'necessary' because the legislation was disproportionate and discriminatory because it did not authorise the detention of British citizens so suspected.

Similarly, in *Bank Mellat v HM Treasury (No 2)* [2013] UKSC 39 a direction restricting the access of an Iranian Bank to UK financial markets was set aside. The Counter Terrorism Act 2008 authorised such restrictions for those reasonably believed to be facilitating the development or production of nuclear weapons in a country where this posed significant risk to the UK's national interests. A bare majority of the nine-judge Supreme Court concluded that the distinction made between Bank Mellat and other Iranian Banks with access to UK financial markets was arbitrary and irrational. This was although they acknowledged (see for example [21] per Lord Sumption, whose extra-judicial views are discussed at 154) that the question whether a measure is apt to limit the risk posed for the national interest by nuclear proliferation 'is pre-eminently a matter for the executive'.

The dissenting judgments in *Bank Mellat* are powerful and compelling. Notwithstanding the applicability of the HRA, Lord Reed stated that 'the risks to our national interests, if the wrong judgment is made in relation to nuclear proliferation, could hardly be more serious' but 'the court did not possess expertise or experience in international relations, national security or financial regulation'. He stated at [129] that since 'democratic responsibility and accountability for protecting the citizens of this country from those risks rest upon the Government, not upon the courts', 'the court has to attach considerable weight to the Government's assessment that the requirements are necessary and proportionate to the risk'. Lord Neuberger at [163]–[164] and Lord Dyson at [200] made similar observations. That approach prevailed in *R (Shamima Begum) v Home Secretary* [2021] UKSC 7. A person born in the UK who had travelled to Syria to join Isis when she was aged 15 was deprived of her British citizenship four years later. The Home Secretary did this because he considered that her return to the UK would present a risk to its national security and was satisfied that the deprivation would not make her stateless. The statelessness issue raises difficult questions because her alternative nationality was Bangladesh, a country with which she had little real connection, and which did not accept her claim to citizenship so that repatriation there was not a foreseeable outcome. But, on the national security assessment, the court considered that, reasons of institutional capacity and of democratic accountability meant (see [70] and [134]) that considerable respect had to be given to the Home Secretary's decision. It referred to *Secretary of State for the Home Department v Rehman* [2001] UKHL 47 at [62] in which Lord Hoffmann stated that the executive's access to special information and expertise in such matters meant that legitimacy for decisions 'can be conferred only by entrusting them to persons responsible to the community through the democratic process', 'persons whom the people have elected and whom they can remove'.

As to prerogative powers, the court's jurisdiction to determine whether a prerogative power exists was recognised over 400 years ago in the *Case of Proclamations* (1611) 12 Co Rep 74, 76. But Blackstone stated in his *Commentaries* vol 1 250, 252 that the discretion conferred by prerogative powers cannot be questioned. It was only in 1984 in *Council of Civil Service Unions v Minister for the Civil Service* [1985] AC 374, 'the *GCHQ* case' that it was recognised that there is jurisdiction to supervise the exercise of a prerogative power. In practice, however, the scope of judicial control over prerogative powers is narrower than that over statutory powers. This is partly because the subject-matter of the prerogative power may concern a matter allocated to the executive (the appointment of ministers and the conduct of foreign affairs) or the legislature (the internal procedures of Parliament) or (see 126) is non-justiciable and not amenable to the judicial process. Also, as in the case of some discretions conferred by statute, the matter may be one over which courts exercise restraint because it is a matter of policy which they are less well equipped to determine than the democratically elected organs of the state.

In the *GCHQ* case, although in principle civil servants working at GCHQ had a right to be consulted before a decision to bar them from belonging to trade unions, the court concluded that it was for the government to decide whether requirements of national security outweighed that right. The extent of the supervisory jurisdiction over prerogative powers, perhaps its high-water mark, was demonstrated in a highly sensitive situation involving the role of the court and the other two branches of the state in *Miller 2 & Cherry* discussed at 13 and 125. An Order in Council made on the advice of the Prime Minister which purported to prorogue Parliament in September 2019 was quashed.

# IV. HENRY VIII CLAUSES

Such clauses give ministers power to amend or repeal Acts of Parliament by delegated legislation with little or no parliamentary scrutiny. They are so named because Henry VIII was 'regarded popularly as the impersonation of executive autocracy' and his preference was to legislate by proclamations made under the Statute of Proclamations 1539 rather than through Parliament: Committee on Ministers' Powers 1932, at 36. They are concerning for both the rule of law and the separation of powers. As to the former, broad framework provisions coupled with power to repeal or amend primary legislation for a wide range of purposes does not foster certainty. Moreover, as the Committee stated, such a power 'is a standing temptation to Ministers and their subordinates ... to be slipshod in the preparatory work before the Bill is introduced in Parliament'. As to the latter, the Committee stated that such clauses are a standing temptation to seize authority which properly belongs to Parliament. It considered that they could only be justified if temporary and limited to the machinery needed to bring the Act containing the clause into force. More recently it has been said that such clauses push at the boundaries of the constitutional principle that only Parliament may amend or repeal primary legislation: HL Constitution Committee, 2010 §4.

The Committee on Ministers' Powers stated that between 1888 and 1929 there were 8 examples of such provisions. In recent years, however, they have grown exponentially and are now an established feature of the law-making process in this country. In 2010 the Ministry of Justice estimated that more than 120 were passed. Since the enactment of the legislation providing for the UK's withdrawal from the EU, there has been substantial further growth in order to transpose parts of EU law to the post-exit day statute book and to specify areas of such law in which the devolved UK legislatures have no competence. Frequently the only justification given for a Henry VIII clause is that 'flexibility' is needed to deal with future changes of circumstances. This reflects 'the Government's desire to future-proof legislation, both in the light of Brexit and the rapidly changing nature of digital technologies [but that] must be balanced against the need for Parliament to scrutinise and, where necessary, constrain executive power': HL Constitution Committee 2018, §§ 64–66.

It is now possible to use Henry VIII clauses for much broader purposes than those envisaged by the Committee on Ministers Powers, going well beyond tidying up. An example is the power in the Legislative and Regulatory Reform Act 2006. Even after significant restrictions were introduced during its passage through Parliament, it empowers the amendment of any legislation to 'reduce any burden' for the purpose of ensuring that regulatory functions are carried out in a 'transparent, accountable, proportionate and consistent' way. It was said (letter to *The Times* 16 February 2006) that the original Bill would have allowed a minister to abolish or curtail jury trial and the Prime Minister to sack judges, and one of the restrictions introduced was that the power cannot be used to enact a provision of 'constitutional significance'.

Henry VIII powers are also found in statutes with a constitutional dimension. For example, the Constitutional Reform and Governance Act 2010, which provides a statutory basis for the management of the civil service, ratification of treaties, Parliamentary Standards, and Freedom of Information, contains a power for ministers to 'amend, repeal or revoke any existing statutory provision'. The power in the Childcare Act 2016 to amend, repeal or revoke any provision made by or under an Act (whenever passed or made) authorises the creation of criminal offences. So, although the strict construction referred to means that a power to vary 'any enactment' only applies to past Acts, this is one of many examples of power to amend legislation passed after the Act conferring the power.

Where power is conferred for a broad range of purposes, as well as very limited or no Parliamentary control, the potential for control by judicial review is narrowed even though courts construe such provisions strictly: *R v Secretary of State for the Environment, ex p Spath Holme Ltd* [2002]

2 AC 349 at [35]. As well as breadth of purposes, such clauses may not be subject to the one-year sunset clause the Committee on Ministers Powers recommended. For example, sections 89 and 90 of the Coronavirus Act 2020 provide for a sunset clause of two years with power to extend it for six months at a time.

This represents a shift by stealth in the balance of constitutional power towards the executive at the expense of the legislature. It also increases uncertainty and creates a potential conflict with rule of law values because it allows primary legislation to be skeletal, containing virtually nothing of substance beyond what has been described as a vague 'mission statement': HL Constitution Committee 2018, § 53. The Constitution Committee referred to a suspicion that such clauses are sometimes used not to 'future-proof' against unforeseen contingencies but because the government has committed itself to doing something but does not know quite what to do, or the policy has not been worked out. It also stated at §67 that these clauses are

> a departure from constitutional principle. Departures from constitutional principle should be contemplated only where a full and clear explanation and justification is provided. Such justification should set out the specific purpose that the Henry VIII power is designed to serve and how the power will be used. Widely drawn delegations of legislative authority cannot be justified solely by the need for speed and flexibility.

At the time of writing there is no sign that government accepts these serious criticisms or will attempt to wean itself off the wide use of framework legislation and Henry VIII clauses. Indeed, the pressures of putting in place legal structures for the UK's complicated future relationship with the EU and EU law, and for dealing with the Covid-19 pandemic have led to a significant increase in their use with very real dangers for the operation of the rule of law. See HL Delegated Powers and Regulatory Reform Committee's 12th Report of Session 2021–22, *Democracy Denied? The urgent need to rebalance power between Parliament and the Executive* 24 November 2021.

# 6

## Access to Justice

This chapter deals with two interlinked components of access to justice. The first is that people should have access to a court or tribunal to defend themselves against criminal charges or to resolve their disputes in a binding manner without undue delay. On the efficacy of attempts to exclude such access, see 144. The second is that the procedures provided by the state should be fair, enabling both parties to put their case. The primary concern here is with courts and tribunals, but the requirements of fairness for administrative decision-making by ministers and other public officials are also touched on. The requirement that the judges resolving those disputes should be independent and impartial is considered in the next chapter. The importance of an independent legal profession with a duty to represent all, including the unpopular, odious and heinous is referred to at 30.

In considering the requirements of the two components, it is important to bear in mind the different purposes served by criminal, civil and public law justice. The state uses criminal law to set out what must not be done, to determine whether individuals have committed crimes, and to punish those who have. Through civil and family law, the state sustains social stability and economic growth. It does so by providing public processes for resolving civil disputes about matters such as contracts, civil wrongs (known as 'torts') and property; and disputes within families, including property rights on divorce and about children. It also provides procedures for enforcing legal rights and for protecting private and personal rights. Public law is concerned with the exercise of constitutional responsibility, ensuring that government and public authorities act in accordance with the law. It does so by two processes. The first is a common law supervisory jurisdiction called 'judicial review', which is concerned with the legality of governmental and public action rather than its merits, although the line between the two can be difficult to draw, see discussion at 58 ff. The second are the statutory rights of appeal or other mechanisms for challenging decisions by public authorities, tailored by reference to context so that areas such as environmental regulation, social security, special educational needs, and immigration have processes specifically adapted for them.

# I. ACCESS TO COURTS AND TRIBUNALS

The origins of the common law right of access to the courts by individuals lie in the statement in clause 40 of the *Magna Carta* of 1215 that 'we will not sell, deny or delay right or justice to anyone'. *Coke's Institutes* 1642 Part II, 55 states that 'every subject of this Realme, for injury done to him … may take his remedy by the course of the Law and have justice … freely without sale, fully without any deniall, and speedily without delay'.

The common law right assumes that there will be sufficient courts, tribunal hearing rooms, judges and staff to dispense justice without delay. The Lord Chancellor is under a statutory duty, now in section 1(1) of the Courts Act 2003 and section 39 of the Tribunals, Courts and Enforcement Act 2007 to ensure that there is an efficient and effective system to support the courts and tribunals and 'to provide appropriate services' for them, including staff and accommodation. The breadth and generality of this duty suggests that it is an aspirational 'target duty' to do one's best so that failure to achieve the statutory goal without more does not constitute a justiciable breach. If, as the Lord Chief Justice stated in May 2020, the administration of justice 'has been underfunded for years and years', and 'the consequences of that underfunding are coming home to roost' (HC Justice Committee 2020, §95) it may be possible to argue that a failure in a particular area has crystallised the duty in that area and made it enforceable: *R (G) v Barnet LBC* [2003] UKHL 208 at [14] and [88]. An efficient and effective court system depends on adequate financing but, as noted below and at 66–67 and 129, there are formidable difficulties in successfully challenging the legality of resource allocation decisions.

Since 2007 there has been direct competition for resources between courts and prisons. A single department, the Ministry of Justice, headed by a single person holding the offices of Lord Chancellor and Secretary of State for Justice, and with a single budget, is responsible for both. There is competition because the more people there are in prisons, the less funding there is for courts and tribunals and for legal aid. The significant retrenchment by the state after the financial crisis in 2008 resulted in these areas all suffering financial cuts. But, in what has been a politically charged process, it has been easier to cut funding for courts. Since 2010 about half the magistrates' courts in England and Wales and some 250 other courts and hearing centres have been closed. Many users have had to travel further to get to the location of their hearing, in rural areas sometimes much further. Those with disabilities and on lower incomes have been disproportionately affected. Challenges to the closures were unsuccessful because in substance they were to the merits of the individual decisions rather than their legality. The high threshold required for a rationality challenge, see 59, was not met. Courts were invited to engage in a comparison of the adequacy of court facilities and buildings, on which reasonable people may differ, or to trespass into the realms of resource allocation which is the business of the democratically accountable institutions of the state rather than the courts: *R (Robin Murray & Co) v Lord Chancellor* [2011] EWHC 1528 (Admin) at [57] and *Vale of Glamorgan Council v Lord Chancellor* [2011] EWHC 1532 (Admin) at [40].

The government considers that the savings achieved from closing underused or sub-standard courts will enable it to improve access to justice by using technology and a digitised court system. But care must be taken not to lose other values of a system where people 'have their day in court' and confront their opponents in public before an independent judge. It is estimated that about 45 per cent of older and vulnerable people are unable to engage digitally with courts and tribunals, and it is essential that promises that no one will have to do so are kept: HC Justice Committee 2019, §§27–28, 40, 2020, §§ 12, 44.

The common law right of access by individuals was emphatically affirmed by the Supreme Court in *R (UNISON) v Lord Chancellor* [2017] UKSC 51. An Order which introduced fees for claims in Employment Tribunals of an amount which had the effect of reducing the number of claims brought by over 66 per cent was held unlawful. The reduction was 'so sharp, so substantial, and so sustained' that the court concluded that a significant number of people who would otherwise have brought claims found the fees to be unaffordable. In a judgment agreed with by the other six members of the Court, Lord Reed stated at [66] that 'the constitutional right of access to the courts is inherent in the rule of law' and at [76], building on the judgment of Laws J in

*R v Lord Chancellor, ex p Witham* [1998] QB 575, that unhindered access 'can only be curtailed by a clear statutory enactment'. There was no such enactment in that case. More recently, it has been said that the common law right of access to justice is 'not a relative right to be balanced against other rights and interests, the convenience of the executive or the courts, or the risks of abuse of process' and outweighed by such factors (*R (FB Afghanistan) v Home Secretary* [2020] EWCA Civ 1338 at [117]) although this may not be so where the other factor is national security: see *R (Shamima Begum) v Home Secretary* [2021] UKSC 7 (discussed at p 68) at [90]–[91] and [135].

The common law right of access is now complemented by the right implicitly contained in the right to a fair and public hearing within a reasonable time before an independent and impartial tribunal set out in ECHR Article 6(1). The Strasbourg Court has described that right as a fundamental principle of the rule of law: *Salabiaku v France* (1988) 13 EHRR 379 at [28]. The right would be illusory unless the legal system also provides those who succeed in court with an effective means of enforcing the judgment. So, a refusal by Greek authorities to comply with judgments for five years was held unlawful: *Hornsby v Greece* (1997) 24 EHRR 250 at [40] and [45].

In civil cases, the importance of access to the courts is, as Lord Reed explained in the *UNISON* case, that without it 'laws are liable to become a dead letter' and because the provision of effective access is not of value only to the particular individuals involved in a case but also to society in general. The knowledge that individuals and businesses are likely to be able to enforce their rights is important in shaping the behaviour both of those whose rights have been infringed and of wrongdoers. Such knowledge promotes clarity and stability: *UNISON* at [68]–[73]. Additionally cases brought by individuals or by prosecution authorities such as those referred to at 44–45, may resolve uncertainty and establish principles of general importance to the wider public which enable people to behave in a way that will avoid disputes arising in the future: Genn 1999, 264 and 2010, 143.

Alternative methods of dispute resolution ('ADR') not involving the state, such as negotiation, mediation and arbitration, are often chosen by parties. They sometimes do so freely, for example because they desire a private and confidential process, and sometimes because of the expense or delay of litigation. Government policy for many years has been to encourage ADR and to reduce the proportion of disputes resolved by litigation. But while free resort to ADR may be a good thing, 'to oblige truly unwilling parties to refer their disputes to mediation would be to impose an unacceptable obstruction on their right of access to the court': *Halsey v Milton Keynes General NHS Trust* [2004] EWCA Civ 576 at [9]. Moreover, the resolution of disputes by ADR processes 'can only work fairly and properly if they are backed up by the knowledge on both sides that a fair and just system of adjudication will be available if they fail': *UNISON* at [72]. The effectiveness of law depends on the messages that come from the courts. It is for this reason that the view of government since 1992 that the civil justice system is not a public good to be provided by it but a service to be paid for by its users through 'full-cost recovery' is so wrong: see the powerful critique by Genn 2010, 46 ff.

The right of access to courts is about access to vindicate rights which exist or can be said on arguable grounds to exist in our law, such as the right to compensation for breaches of contract or for unlawful detention. It is not a right to assert that individuals should have a substantive right which it is clear that they do not have, for example rights that exist in other countries, such as under New Zealand's no-fault compensation scheme for personal injuries: *Matthews v Ministry of Defence* [2003] UKHL 4 at [24]–[25]. The presence or absence of a substantive right is generally properly the province of government and Parliament rather than the courts. But where a substantive right arguably exists, procedural barriers or practical impediments restricting its effective exercise, such as time limits, the provision of security for costs and the other barriers discussed below must be justified.

Whether the absence of a substantive right poses a difficulty for the rule of law because the right is considered essential to the life and dignity of individuals in a democratic society raises different issues to those considered in this chapter and is considered in chapters 2 and 9. At this stage, it should be noted that the distinction between substance and procedure can be 'a slippery one' which is difficult to draw. Moreover, some substantive rules which can be described as conferring immunity on a particular class of defendants may be perceived as objectionable restrictions on a claimant's right of access to the court: *Matthews v Ministry of Defence* at [33] and [129]. The Strasbourg Court so regarded the rule of English law that no action lies against the police for alleged negligence in conducting criminal investigations in *Osman v UK* (1998) 29 EHRR 245 but largely resiled three years later. In *Z v UK* (2001) 34 EHRR 97 it stated that *Osman* was based on a misunderstanding of the English law of negligence. The Strasbourg jurisprudence recognises that it may not create by way of Article 6(1) a substantive legal right which has no basis in the state concerned. In *A v UK* (2003) 36 EHRR 51 at [63] it, however, stated that

> it would not be consistent with the rule of law in a democratic society, or with the basic principle underlying Art. 6(1) – namely that civil claims must be capable of being submitted to a judge for adjudication – if a state could, without restraint or control ... remove from the jurisdiction of the courts a whole range of civil claims or confer immunities from civil liability on large groups or categories of persons.

The controversial question of whether the right of access to a court can be totally excluded is discussed at 144 and see 44. But whatever the answer to that, it follows from Parliamentary sovereignty that the right of access is not absolute, and it has been limited in various ways. Vexatious litigants, compulsorily detained mental patients and those wishing to bring judicial review claims against public bodies are required to obtain the consent of the High Court before commencing proceedings. There are time limits for bringing claims, and immunities protect certain bodies and individuals. The immunities include those conferred by Article IX of the Bill of Rights 1689 on proceedings in Parliament and the exclusive cognisance or jurisdiction of each House of Parliament to regulate its own affairs free of outside interference. Judges are immune from suit for a judicial act even where (see 102) malice is alleged, although judges of inferior courts are not immune for acts outside their jurisdiction: *Re MC (A minor)* [1985] AC 528, 541 and Shetreet and Turenne §§7.2–7.4. The immunity of the sovereign acts of a foreign state from suit in English Courts against its will is now subject to wide-ranging exceptions under the State Immunity Act 1978 but is still significant. Additionally, the level of court fees, requirements for security for costs, and the cost of obtaining legal advice and representation may impose practical impediments to access for all but the wealthy.

The robustness of the protection given to the right of access is illustrated by *Chester v Bateson* [1920] 1KB 829. A regulation promulgated during World War I made it a criminal offence for a landlord to commence proceedings to evict munition workers without the consent of the Minister of Munitions was held invalid. The Court stated that such a grave invasion of rights could only be done by primary legislation, and then only by express words. As was stated by Lord Hoffmann in *Matthews v Ministry of Defence* at [28]:

> A right to the independence and impartiality of the judicial branch of government would not be worth much if the executive branch could stop you from

getting to the court in the first place. The executive would in effect be deciding the case against you. That would contravene the rule of law and the principle of the separation of powers.

Even where the right of access has been curtailed by clear and express statutory words, its degree must not be greater than is reasonably necessary to meet the statutory objectives which legitimately justify it, and must not impair the essence of the right: *Anderton v Clwyd CC* [2002] 1 WLR 3174 at [31]. In short, the restriction must be proportionate. For example, the power of the court to require a litigant to provide security for the costs of the other party before proceeding cannot be exercised in a way that would unfairly stifle a claim or an appeal, see *Ali v Keith Hudson* [2003] EWCA Civ 1793 at [40].

Many of the restrictions on access can be justified as ways of serving legitimate aims in a proportionate way. The filter for vexatious litigants is justified because they have abused the right of access in the past by bringing many hopeless cases. For mental patients who can only claim against staff working with them for acts done in bad faith or without reasonable care, the justification is to protect the staff from being unduly targeted: *Seal v Chief Constable of South Wales* [2007] UKHL 31. Similarly, permission to appeal is required in most cases and is justified as filtering out civil cases in which there is no realistic prospect of success, and criminal cases where it is not arguable that a conviction is unsafe or that a sentence is manifestly excessive, wrong in principle, or not lawful.

The limitation periods imposed by the Limitation Act 1980 are justified by the need to ensure legal certainty and finality, and because they do not reduce access to such an extent that its essence is impaired. They protect defendants from stale claims which are difficult to counter, particularly where the evidence is unreliable or incomplete because of the passage of time: *Stebbings v Webb* [1993] AC 498; *Stebbings v UK* (1997) 23 EHRR 213. The requirement that judicial review claims be brought promptly and in any event within three months, is justified by the need for public authorities and third parties relying on their decisions not to be kept in suspense as to their legal validity.

Other procedural rules such as those to ensure the effectiveness of freezing orders or imposing sanctions for non-compliance have been held to be justified if fair. Parties who neither comply, nor seek an extension of the period or relief against the sanctions are not denied access because of the rule but because of their own non-compliance: *Stolzenberg v CIBC Mellon Trust Co Ltd* [2004] EWCA Civ 827 at [161].

The reasons that state immunity and parliamentary immunity are not disproportionate restrictions on access to the courts are based respectively on the rules of customary international law and constitutional propriety and separation of powers. State immunity is not a self-imposed procedural limitation on the jurisdiction of its courts which the UK has chosen to adopt. It is a rule of international law derived from the equality and independence of sovereign states which is imposed on all states, with no exception for claimants alleging torture: *Matthews v Ministry of Defence* at [104]. All states are obliged to comply with this rule and 'a state cannot deny access to its court if it has no access to give': *Jones v Ministry of the Interior of Saudi Arabia* [2006] UKHL 26 at [14].

Article IX of the Bill of Rights 1689 confers absolute immunity for 'proceedings in Parliament' freeing MPs from the risk of prosecution by government and from civil proceedings by others for what they say in Parliament. The Strasbourg Court has held this to be justified by two legitimate aims: protecting free speech in Parliament, especially important for elected representatives, and maintaining the separation of powers between the legislature and the judiciary. In *A v UK* (2003) 36 EHRR 51 an MP 'named and shamed' individuals in his constituency he considered were 'neighbours from hell' by making what the Strasbourg Court described as 'extremely serious and clearly unnecessary' allegations in a debate on housing policy. The Court recognised that the broader an immunity is, the more compelling the justification must be, but for two reasons concluded that absolute immunity was proportionate. The first, that the immunity of statements made in Parliament is designed to protect the interests of Parliament as a whole, not the personal interests of individual members, was difficult to maintain while section 13 of the Defamation Act 1996 (repealed in 2015) enabled an MP to waive the protection. The second is also open to question because it is doubtful how effective the ability of victims of defamatory misstatements in Parliament to petition the House to secure a retraction or the power of Parliament to punish a deliberately misleading statement as a contempt would be. The important safeguard is that it is for the Court, paying regard to the views of Parliament, and not Parliament itself to determine the scope of parliamentary privilege. In *R v Chaytor* [2010] UKSC 52 the Supreme Court held that neither article IX nor the exclusive cognisance were a bar to the jurisdiction of the Crown Court to try MPs charged with false accounting of their claims for parliamentary expenses.

Turning to practical impediments to access, administrative rules and practices which significantly impede the ability of those in prison to institute legal proceedings have been held unlawful. Examples include requiring the Home Secretary's consent, an internal investigation or a complaint before forwarding an application or permitting a prisoner to consult a lawyer: *Golder v UK* (1975) 1 EHRR 524 at [26] and [36]; *Raymond v Honey* [1983] 1 AC 1, 13, 14 and *R v Home Secretary, ex p Anderson* [2000] QB 778. Rules and practices which infringe the confidentiality of communications with lawyers, or impede prisoners seeking to gain access to justice via an investigative journalist have also been held unlawful: *R v Home Secretary, ex p Leech* [1994] QB 198 and *R (Daly) v Home Secretary* [2001] UKHL 26; and *R v Home Secretary, ex p Simms* [2000] 2 AC 115.

As seen in the *UNISON* case, court fees may also in practice deny access to justice. Lord Reed stated that a Fees Order would be unlawful 'if there is a real risk that persons will effectively be prevented from having access to justice'. 'In order for court fees to be lawful they have to be set at a level that everyone can afford, taking into account the availability of full or partial remission'. In that case there was very limited remission and no statutory authority. Even if there had been, the court considered that the degree of intrusion was greater than was justified by the statutory objective of making resources available for the justice system. It stated that 'where households on low to middle incomes can only afford to pay fees by sacrificing the ordinary and reasonable expenditure required to maintain an acceptable standard of living, the fees cannot be regarded as affordable'. It also stated that fees can prevent access to justice 'if they render it futile or irrational to bring a claim'. The fees might make it futile to claim where the claimant was for example seeking a non-financial benefit such as regular work-breaks or the right to join a trade union, or seeking only a modest financial award.

Finally, there is the cost of legal advice and representation. There is an overlap between any requirements of the right of access to the courts in relation to legal aid and the common law duty of procedural fairness embodying the principles of natural justice. This is because even if the cost of advice and representation mean that individuals decide to institute proceedings without it, if the absence of advice or representation means they are not able to participate and conduct their cases effectively, the procedure will be unfair: *Osborn v Parole Board* [2013] UKSC 61 at [89]. Lord Reed stated at [55] that this protection is not a distinct area based on the case law of the Strasbourg court but 'permeates our legal system'.

Courts recognise that a wide margin is to be allowed to government in the allocation of limited resources, including legal aid, because such allocation is generally within the constitutional competence of the legislature or executive rather than the courts. It has therefore been stated that there is no constitutional right to legal assistance at public expense: *R (Sisangia) v Director of Legal Aid Casework* [2016] EWCA Civ 24 at [8]–[9], applying Laws J in *R v Lord Chancellor, ex p Witham* [1998] QB 575 at 586. This position is difficult to reconcile with the recognition (see 80) that practical impediments can cause a serious hinderance to the right of access to the court and that the complexity of a case may render the right of access illusory and ineffective without legal representation.

Legal aid has been provided by statute since the Poor Persons Act 1903. It is now governed by the Legal Aid, Sentencing and Punishment of Offenders Act 2012 ('LASPO 2012'). ECHR Article 6(3)(c) requires those charged with a criminal offence to be given free legal assistance if they have not got sufficient means, when the interests of justice require it, which they do if deprivation of liberty is at stake: *Benham v UK* (1996) 22 EHRR 293 at [64]. In broad terms the criteria for determining whether legal aid is required are similar for criminal and civil cases. But, whereas for criminal cases the service is 'demand led', the introduction of a fixed budget for legal aid by what has been described as the 'interestingly named' Access to Justice Act 1999 has led to serious reductions in civil legal aid: Genn 2010, 39.

The test for this aspect of the right of access is whether, without legal aid, litigants are able to present their cases effectively and have effective involvement in the decision-making process. That will depend on the particular facts and circumstances of each case. In both criminal and civil cases the factors include: (a) the financial means of the litigant, (b) the importance of the issues at stake; (c) the complexity of the procedural, legal and evidential issues; and (d) the ability of the individual to represent herself without legal assistance, having regard to her age, mental capacity and language skills: see *R (Gudanaviciene) v Director of Legal Aid Casework and Lord Chancellor* [2014] EWCA Civ 1622; *Benham v UK* (1996) 22 EHRR 293 at [60]–[63] and LASPO 2012, section 17.

In *Steel & Morris v UK* (2005) 41 EHRR 22, the Strasbourg Court held that the complexity and length of libel proceedings against two environmental campaigners who had produced a leaflet entitled 'What's the connection between McDonald's and starvation in the Third World?' violated their right to a fair trial principally because of the unavailability of legal aid for defamation cases. The circumstances were extreme. The trial with 130 oral witnesses, including a number of experts dealing with a range of scientific questions, lasted 313 court days, including 100 days of legal argument and the appeal hearing lasted 23 days. In *R (Howard League) v Lord Chancellor* [2017] EWCA Civ 244, the decision to remove certain Parole Board reviews and two other areas of decision-making concerning prisoners from the scope of the criminal legal aid scheme was held to create inherent or systemic unfairness. Many prisoners would be unable to participate effectively in procedures involving some complex questions of law and procedure, and the assessment of difficult questions of risk assessment and prediction in psychiatric and psychological evidence.

It is important also to consider whether effective participation can be enabled by alternatives to legal aid. These include conditional fee agreements which pass the financial risk to a person's lawyers and persuading a lawyer to act *pro bono*. In the *Howard League* case, the court acknowledged that there might have been safeguards other than legal aid which would have enabled prisoners to participate effectively. But it concluded that the evidence showed that neither the inquisitorial nature of Parole Board procedures and the Board's expertise, nor the other alternatives relied on by the Lord Chancellor, such as assistance by specialist charities and prison staff, were adequate, particularly for vulnerable prisoners such as those with learning difficulties or mental illness. In *Steel & Morris*, the limited and sporadic *pro bono* help received, and the extensive assistance and latitude granted by the court was no substitute for competent and sustained representation by an experienced lawyer.

## II. FAIR PROCEDURES

The right to a fair trial or hearing is fundamental and absolute, but it is accepted that what a fair trial requires cannot be 'the subject of a single, unwavering rule or collection of rules' and that 'it is proper to take account of the facts and circumstances of particular cases': see for example *Brown v Stott* [2003] 1 AC 681, at 693 and *A v UK* (2009) 49 EHRR 625 at [203].

This is vividly illustrated by the fact that although Lord Devlin 1956, 164, stated that trial by jury is 'more than an instrument of justice and more than one wheel of the constitution: it is the lamp that shows that freedom lives', only those charged with a serious crime have the right to trial by jury. Even then, where there is a real and present danger of jury tampering, and it is not practicable to make arrangements to prevent it without unreasonable intrusion on the lives of the jury, there is power to try an accused without a jury: Criminal Justice Act 2003, sections 44–49. Jury trial has virtually disappeared in civil proceedings.

Procedural fairness can thus be achieved in a variety of ways. The parties must have what the Strasbourg jurisprudence refers to as 'equality of arms', a fair balance between them, giving each a reasonable opportunity to present their case under conditions which do not put that party at a substantial disadvantage compared to their opponent. At one end of the procedural spectrum are adversarial procedures in which the decision maker is essentially a referee between the disputing parties who themselves choose and present the issues. At the other end are inquisitorial procedures in which the decision maker is actively involved in investigating the facts and identifying the relevant legal questions. Additionally, there is more informal decision-making by government ministers, civil servants, and other public officials that may have significant impact on rights or interests.

One of the hallmarks of common law court procedures has been that, save for contexts such as the welfare of children, they are primarily adversarial. But over the last 30 years a significant inquisitorial element has been added by the extensive case management powers given to and used by judges. Decision-making by tribunals and public officials was traditionally far more informal and inquisitorial. However, tribunals have become more like courts since the 2001 Leggatt Review of the Tribunal System. In 2006 a single Tribunal Service with shared procedural rules supplemented by jurisdiction specific ones for particular tribunals was set up and, in 2011, a unified Court and Tribunal Service ('HMCTS') was created. Since 2015 proposals for online proceedings contemplate further departures from the adversarial process. The catalysts may have been the effect of austerity on the justice system and the view of HM Treasury that a digitised court system would be cheaper. But the effect may be to increase access to justice in low-value civil cases if the promises are kept that the approximately 45 per cent of older and vulnerable people who are unable to engage digitally with courts and tribunals will not have to do so: Susskind 2019, 146–47.

Wherever on the spectrum a procedure lies, there is a fundamental common law right to participate in proceedings in accordance with the principles of open justice and natural justice. The wider public interest in the open justice principle has been discussed at 50. For the parties to a case, it is difficult to separate it from the principles of natural justice. These entitle people to adequate notice of the case against them and the evidence on which it is based, and adequate time to prepare and present their own case before an independent and impartial judge. Both principles also normally require a court to provide a reasoned decision so the parties know why they have won or lost and can decide whether to appeal.

In criminal cases, accused persons have the right to be present at the trial save where they waive it by absconding or misbehaving. Similarly, the judge can only exceptionally permit a trial to continue in the absence of an accused who is unrepresented, and his summing up to the jury must expose weaknesses in the prosecution case and warn them that absence is not an admission of guilt: *R v Hayward* [2001] EWCA Crim 168 at [22], affirmed *sub nom R v Jones* [2002] UKHL 5 at [13]. The presumption of innocence, requiring the prosecution to prove beyond reasonable doubt that a person is guilty, provides a substantive dimension to the protection of the accused. The result is that reverse burdens of proof have to be compellingly justified, for example where the matter is one which relates to facts which, if they exist, are readily provable by the defendant as within his own knowledge or to which he has ready access: *Lambert* [2001] UKHL 37 at [34] and [40] and *Sheldrake v DPP* [2004] UKHL 43 at [40]–[41].

Although administrative decisions are made by ministers and other public officials or bodies rather than independent judges, they are also subject to the rules of natural justice. These were significantly strengthened by *Ridge v Baldwin* [1964] AC 40, a case where a chief constable who was acquitted of conspiracy to obstruct justice was then dismissed without being given an opportunity to put his side of the case. What procedural fairness requires is acutely sensitive to the fact that Parliament has entrusted the decision to the minister or other public official or body, and the context. The need is for flexible safeguards that avoid a skeletal version of the elaborate rules of court and tribunal procedure and over-formality and over-judicialisation: *R (L) v West London Mental Health NHS Trust* [2014] EWCA Civ 47 at [67] ff. There is broad consensus about the factors affecting what is required in a particular context: see *Lloyd v McMahon* [1987] AC 625, 702; *R v Home Secretary, ex p Doody* [1994] 1 AC 531, 560 and *R (Howard League) v Lord Chancellor* [2017] EWCA Civ 244 at [39]. These include the nature of the function under consideration, the statutory or other framework in which the decision-maker operates, the circumstances in which action may be taken, the breadth of the discretion granted, and the range of decisions open to the decision-maker. They also include the interest of the person affected, the consequences of the decision for that person's rights or interests, and whether the process has a 'rationing' aspect of scarce resources available, for example for legal aid, health care, housing and policing. Considerations of urgency or confidentiality will limit what fairness requires in a particular case, as will the fact that a decision is a non-dispositive preliminary decision by an investigating body. Where there is no right to appeal an administrative decision the remedy is to challenge its legality in judicial review proceedings.

Court and tribunal rules ensure that adequate notice and time to prepare is generally given but there are exceptions. For example, a summons served in the morning to appear at a magistrates' court that afternoon gave the accused inadequate time to prepare and the resulting conviction was quashed: *R v Thames JJ, ex p Polemis* [1974] 1 WLR 1372, 1375. A detention fast track system which required tribunals to hear appeals of those detained in the system within seven days of the refusal of their application for asylum was held unlawful because the time limits were so tight as to make it impossible for there to be a fair hearing of appeals in a significant number of cases: *R (Detention Action) v Home Secretary* [2015] EWCA Civ 840 at [45].

Notwithstanding the Magna Carta and ECHR Article 6(1), delay has long been a significant obstacle to access to justice in civil proceedings. As described by Charles Dickens in *Bleak House*, in Victorian times interminable delays were caused by procedural complexity and the time taken for decisions to be made. Despite the implementation of Lord Woolf's 1996 *Access to Justice* report, and the introduction of a proactive system of case management and encouragement of settlement by ADR, delay remains a problem today because of the increasing complexity of litigation and the years of underfunding: HC Justice Committee 2020, §95, evidence of LCJ. In the last quarter of 2019 fast and multi-track county court cases for claims of respectively under £25,000 and over £25,000 took an average of over a year to reach trial, exceeding the upper limit of the target: Civil Justice Statistics Quarterly, 7. The Crown Court backlog rose by 13 per cent to 37,434 cases: HC Justice Committee 2020, §12. In 2020, as a result of the pandemic, despite heroic efforts by judges and court staff in the under-resourced system, the Crown Court backlog increased by over 31 per cent to over 53,000 with some trials pushed back to 2023.

In criminal cases the court has the power to stay prosecutions on the ground of delay but the threshold is high because of the public interest in the final determination of criminal charges: *A-G's Reference (No 2 of 2001)* [2003] UKHL 68 at [22]. Only when a lesser remedy will not enable a fair trial or where a compelling reason means that it would be unfair to try the accused should a prosecution be stayed. The Strasbourg jurisprudence on the right in ECHR Article 6(1) to a hearing within a reasonable time makes it clear that 'contracting states cannot blame unacceptable delays on the general want of prosecutors or judges or courthouses or on chronic underfunding of the legal system': *Dyer v Watson* [2004] 1 AC 379 at [55]. In deciding whether a delay is unacceptable, courts are, however, entitled to take account of the practical reality of litigation even in a reasonably well organised system. This includes the complexity of the case, whether the accused is in custody or not, and whether the delay has been caused by his own conduct.

In civil cases proceedings are started by issuing a claim form. But since the 1996 reforms, parties are encouraged (ultimately by the risk of a costs penalty or the refusal of publicly funded representation) to resolve their disputes by providing information in what are known as letters before claim and using ADR procedures such as mediation. Diversion to settlement by pre-action protocols in areas such as personal injuries, judicial review and housing can be seen as a form of outsourcing to non-state dispute resolution, a form of 'privatisation'. There are implications for this aspect of the rule of law if, as some suggest, informal ADR processes can increase the power of the stronger party behind a façade of the neutrality of the mediator: see the discussion of the different views by Genn 2010, 90–91, 112–13 and 124 and Galligan, 276–79. Moreover, when ADR is used, a private and generally confidential process replaces public justice which, as noted at 76–77, is a public good with purposes that include, but go beyond, providing the service of dispute resolution.

In both civil and criminal cases, parties are required to disclose their cases in advance. In criminal cases the accused must be told of the grounds for the arrest at the time or as soon as is practicable afterwards: *Christie v Leachinsky* [1947] AC 573; Police and Criminal Evidence Act 1984, section 28; and ECHR Articles 5(2) and 6(3)(a). The police must record and reveal material obtained during a criminal investigation to the prosecution which is itself under a continuing duty to disclose relevant documents to the defence. In *R v H* [2004] UKHL 3 at [14] it was stated that:

Fairness ordinarily requires that any material held by the prosecution which weakens its case or strengthens that of the defendant, if not relied on as part of its formal case against the defendant, should be disclosed to the defence. Bitter experience has shown that miscarriages of justice may occur where such material is withheld from disclosure. The golden rule is that full disclosure of such material should be made.

Defendants must furnish a defence statement setting out the nature of the defence, the matters of fact in dispute with the prosecution, particulars of any alibi, any points of law to be relied on and identifying the witnesses to be called: Criminal Procedure and Investigations Act 1996, sections 5, 6A, 6C, 6D.

In civil cases the position has been described as a 'cards on the table' approach: *Davies v Eli Lilly* [1987] 1 WLR 428, 432. Parties must set out their cases in 'pleadings' and must exchange the statements made by those who are to be witnesses. An important element in ensuring equality of arms is that parties are also required to disclose to each other relevant documents (including encrypted electronic data) on which they will rely or which will adversely affect their case which can be located by a reasonable search that is proportionate to the nature and complexity of the case: CPR 31.6 and 31.7(1). It has been said that 'it would be artificial and undesirable for the actual evidence which is relevant and admissible, not to be placed before the judge who is trying the case': *Jones v University of Warwick* [2003] EWCA Civ 151 at [28]. For this reason, there are also processes for a party to obtain evidence by compulsion from non-parties who, through no fault of their own, get mixed up in the acts of the other party so as to facilitate the alleged wrong, where this is necessary and proportionate. For example, a ticket resale website was required to disclose the identity of those who anonymously advertised tickets for rugby matches at Twickenham at inflated prices, in breach of their contracts with the RFU: *The Rugby Football Union v Consolidated Information Services Ltd* [2012] UKSC 55.

Those accused of crimes have rights under the common law and ECHR Article 6(3)(d) to know the identity of their accusers, and to challenge and test their evidence: see *Davis* [2008] UKHL 36 at [5]–[9] for the history. Statutory protection enabling vulnerable witnesses such as children, those with an incapacity and complainants in sex cases to give their evidence remotely or behind screens is not inconsistent with this right. It is necessary to balance the rights of the accused against those of the witnesses. The position of the accused is protected by enabling defence counsel or an intermediary to challenge the witness in cross-examination. The far more difficult problem of balancing the interests of witnesses who are only willing to give evidence anonymously against those of the accused in a way which consistent with the interests of justice and fairness to the accused is discussed at 92–94.

The common law rule excluding hearsay evidence addresses the dangers of admitting evidence that cannot be tested by cross-examination because the witness does not attend the trial at all. But the exceptions to that rule led to a difference between the Strasbourg Court and English courts, now happily resolved. The result is that admitting such evidence may exceptionally be compatible with the rule of law's requirement of fairness even where it is the sole or decisive evidence in a case: *Horncastle* [2009] EWCA Crim 964, [2009] UKSC 14 and *Al-Khawaja & Tahery v UK* (2012) 54 EHRR 23. Two requirements must be satisfied. First, there must be a good reason for the witness's absence. The permitted reasons listed in section 116 of the Criminal Justice Act 2003 are that the witness has died, is abroad or unfit to attend court, cannot be found, or does not give evidence because of a proven 'fear'. Secondly, there must be sufficient safeguards to ensure that no injustice to the defendant results from admitting the evidence. This may be so where it is either not unreliable or where its reliability can realistically be assessed. Examples include business records, confessions, and where the evidence is video-recorded and can be played to the jury. In *Horncastle* [2009] EWCA Crim 964 at [61]–[62] the Court of Appeal gave several other examples, including that of a witness to a drive-by shooting who later dies or is too terrified to give evidence but has noted down the number of the car, which is traced and linked to the defendant.

The principal exceptions to obligations to disclose relevant evidence and documents are where the privilege against self-incrimination or legal professional privilege apply and where the court accepts a claim of 'public interest immunity', that is that disclosure would be injurious to the public interest. Subject to these well-established exceptions, and to the more problematic provisions for 'closed material hearings' which are discussed at 94–95, relevant material cannot be withheld. This is so even if disclosing it would put a party in breach of the criminal law of a foreign state (*Secretary of State for Health v Servier* [2013] EWCA Civ 1234) or it is sensitive and confidential as communications between doctor and patient or journalists and their sources are. But courts have discretion to take other steps to protect confidential information. They may, for example, excuse a witness from answering, redact (that is, obscure) parts of a document which are irrelevant to the issues, or prevent harassment by only permitting the other party's solicitor to inspect documents: *Church of Scientology v DHSS* [1979] 1 WLR 723.

The privilege against self-incrimination means that no one is bound to answer any question or provide information if the effect would have a tendency to expose that person to any criminal charge or penalty under the law of any part of the UK which is reasonably likely to be pursued: *S & A* [2008] EWCA Crim 2177 at [16]; Civil Evidence Act 1968, section 14(1). Described as a 'basic freedom' in *Re Arrows (No 4)* [1995] 2 AC 75 at 95, it goes back to the abolition of the Court of Star Chamber in 1641, a court regarded as an instrument of absolute monarchy. The privilege was a reaction to the unpopularity and openness to abuse of the procedure in that court of subjecting those charged with an offence to interrogation under oath: see Williams, 41. It is subject to at least 25 statutory exceptions: see *Phillips v News Group Newspapers* [2012] UKSC 28 at [11]. But as a result of the decision of the Strasbourg Court in *Saunders v UK* (1996) 23 EHRR 313 most, but not all, of the exceptions now provide that information obtained compulsorily cannot be used in criminal proceedings, save for prosecutions for perjury or, where statute requires a person to answer questions, for failure to do so: Youth Justice and Criminal Evidence Act 1999 sections 58–59.

Legal professional privilege, which goes back to at least the sixteenth century, has been described as a fundamental right only to be statutorily overridden by express words or necessary implication: *R (Morgan Grenfell & Co Ltd) v Special Commissioner of Income Tax* [2002] UKHL 21 at [7]–[8]. It exists to ensure full and frank communications between client and lawyer which promotes broader public interests in the observance of law and administration of justice: *R (Prudential plc) v Special Commissioner of Income Tax* [2013] UKSC 1 at [21] and see [23] and [115] ff. This is because it enables the client to speak without inhibition or holding back half the truth, and it allows the lawyer 'to give honest and candid advice on a sound factual basis' without either of them fearing that the communications may be relied on by an opponent: *R v Derby Magistrates Court, ex p B* [1996] AC 487, 507. These cases and *Three Rivers DC v Bank of England (No 6)* [2004] UKHL 48 make it clear that the privilege is absolute because the rule of law requires citizens to be able to ascertain their legal positions. Whereas other confidential relations, such as those between doctor and patient, can be overridden by some greater public interest such as the needs of public safety, or for the innocent to be acquitted and the guilty convicted, legal professional privilege cannot.

Public interest immunity is a principle of substantive or constitutional law to protect material the production of which would be prejudicial to the public interest. The categories of public interest which are to be weighed against the rights of the party from whom material is to be withheld are not closed. But they include prejudice to national security, communications between states, the workings of central government or the public service, police methods of investigating crime (for example surveillance techniques), confidentiality (for example a journalist's sources), and the identity of informers. Its foundations can be found in *Conway v Rimmer* [1968] AC 910 and *R v Lewes Justices, ex p Home Secretary* [1973] AC 388. Those cases interred the remaining vestiges of what had been known as 'Crown privilege' under which it was believed that only a government minister could apply for evidence to be withheld on this ground and that the minister's decision that evidence should be withheld was absolutely binding. Although applications are still often made by the responsible minister, anyone may apply, and the trial judge may raise the question if no one else has done so. Claims to immunity are now investigated by the court, if necessary, by examining the documents. The harm to the public interest if material is disclosed is balanced against the public interest that the administration of justice should not be frustrated by withholding material. The court will consider whether the material must be produced for justice to be done, taking account of its evidential value.

The process for determining a claim for public interest immunity departs from the adversarial nature of proceedings. In such cases, one party will only know the category of the material to be withheld or, if knowing that would reveal the information, will not know that. In some cases, it may even be necessary not to reveal that an application is being made. It is therefore necessary to proceed with great caution. The court must assess whether the material really helps the party who has not seen it and whether that party's interest can be protected in other ways, for instance by including a summary of the material giving its 'gist' and appointing a person, usually called a 'special advocate', to challenge and test the submissions of the party seeking to withhold the evidence. In criminal proceedings, if no or limited disclosure renders the trial process viewed as a whole unfair then fuller disclosure should be ordered even if this leads the prosecution to discontinue the proceedings in order to avoid having to make disclosure: *R v H* [2004] UKHL 3.

In principle the position in civil proceedings should be the same. But *Carnduff v Rock* [2001] EWCA Civ 680 suggests that is not so. A successful claim to public interest immunity by the defendant, resulted in a claim by a police informer for payment being struck out as untriable because without the evidence the claimant could not establish his case. Although personal liberty is not at stake in civil proceedings, if a fair trial could only take place with disclosure, why should that not be ordered as it is in criminal cases? The justification for the result in *Carnduff's* case may be that a claim for payment by a police informer is not justiciable: Zuckerman §19.30 and *R (Shamima Begum) v Home Secretary* [2021] UKSC 7 (discussed at 68) at [92]–[93].

The statement in *Al Rawi v Security Service* [2011] UKSC 34 that the public interest immunity procedure respects the common law principles of open justice and respect for natural justice may be over-optimistic. *Al Rawi* was a civil claim for damages for complicity in the claimant's extraordinary rendition and illegal detention in Guantánamo Bay in which *Carnduff's* case was considered and discussed without disapproval. Nevertheless, Lord Dyson stated at [41]:

> if documents are disclosed as a result of the process, they are available to both parties and to the court. If they are not disclosed, they are available neither to the other parties nor to the court. Both parties are entitled to full participation in all aspects of the litigation. There is no unfairness or inequality of arms.

It is difficult to reconcile this with *Carnduff's* case where the claimant was unable to have access to material which might have been crucial to establishing his case.

The threats to national security since the attacks by terrorists in the USA on 11 September 2001, the four bombings in London in July 2005 and the long-standing problem of witness intimidation have raised the question whether, in such circumstances, further departures from the principles of open justice and natural justice are compatible with rule of law principles. In *Davis* [2008] UKHL 36, the only witnesses who identified the accused as the person who shot two men dead wished to give evidence anonymously because they feared for their lives. In *Al Rawi's* case the security service claimed it could not defend the claim without relying on some 140,000 documents containing national security material, and those documents could not be considered by the court if it successfully claimed public interest immunity.

When, if at all, should witnesses who fear that they would be harmed by those charged with serious criminal offences or their associates be permitted to give their evidence anonymously? When, if at all, should courts conduct closed material hearings in which sensitive national security material relied on by one party is put before the court but not disclosed to the other party or his lawyers?

Prosecutors and the security service consider that anonymity and closed procedures may be necessary to achieve substantial justice and a fairer trial than would otherwise be possible. If a witness who is frightened does not give evidence, a dangerous criminal may go free. If the government is not able to pursue or defend a case which depends on secret material it faces a dilemma. It either discloses the material, or summaries of it, with consequent damage to the national interest, or it abandons or settles a case which should have been won but cannot be because large amounts of relevant material are not before the court. Additionally, because the court has not been able to consider all the evidence, the parties and the wider public will not have findings about serious allegations: see the 2011 *Justice and Security Green Paper*. It is said that the combination of an independent judge, who sees all the witnesses and material, and a system of security cleared 'special advocates', who take instructions from the excluded party before having access to the closed material and then represent that party's interests at closed hearings with no further contact with the excluded party, are sufficient safeguards.

The Strasbourg court has held that restricting the right to disclosure of relevant evidence including the identity of a witness may be justified when strictly necessary in the light of a strong countervailing public interest such as national security, the need to keep police methods of investigating crime secret, or the fundamental rights of another person: *A v UK* (2009) 49 EHRR 29 at [205]. It has also held that use of a special advocate sufficiently counterbalances the difficulties caused to the person who has not seen the material where either that person is given sufficient information about the allegations to enable him to give effective instructions to the special advocate or where using a closed procedure is proportionate and the proceedings as a whole are fair: *A v UK* at [219]–[220] and *Kennedy v UK* (2011) 52 EHRR 4 at [184] ff.

Notwithstanding the Strasbourg jurisprudence, *Davis* and *Al Rawi* decided that the fundamentality to the common law of the principle of natural justice meant that the court itself could not exercise its inherent power to regulate its own procedure so as to deny a party of the right to participate in proceedings in accordance with that principle. The position differed from the court-created departures from the principle of open justice in hearings and judgments from which the public and the press are excluded to protect children and commercially valuable secret information discussed at 51. In those cases, the parties take full part in the hearing and the judgment is made available to them. Accordingly, *Davis* at [27]–[28] and [45] and *Al Rawi* at [31] and [48] held that it was for Parliament to decide whether anonymous witnesses should give evidence and that closed hearings be allowed and, if so, to devise an appropriate system which still ensured a fair trial. The courts' conclusion in *Al Rawi* was reinforced by the fact that at that time statutes had authorised closed proceedings and the use of special advocates in particular situations including cases before the Special Immigration Appeals Commission and the Investigatory Powers Tribunal.

Parliament reacted swiftly to these decisions. A provision enabling witnesses to give evidence anonymously came into force 33 days after the decision in *Davis* and is now in section 88 of the Coroners and Justice Act 2009. The witness must have real grounds to fear death or injury to himself or another person, or serious danger to property. The court must also be satisfied that, in all the circumstances of the case, granting anonymity is consistent with the accused receiving a fair trial. Section 90 requires the judge to warn the jury not to make any assumptions adverse to the accused and of the difficulties facing a person seeking to challenge the credibility or accuracy of an anonymous witness.

As to national security, the Justice and Security Act 2013 permits closed material proceedings in civil proceedings if a party to the proceedings would be required to disclose material which if disclosed would damage national security. It defines the conditions for doing so in detail. In particular, as well as the provisions for keeping the need for closed proceedings under continual review, there is express provision in section 14(2)(c) to secure compliance with ECHR Article 6. For example, Afghan nationals, who asserted they were covert intelligence sources entitled to be relocated to safe areas and to compensation for loss of employment, were entitled to have whatever disclosure was necessary to enable them to have the 'fair hearing' required by Article 6: *R(K) v Defence Secretary* [2016] EWCA Civ 1149.

Closed material procedures remain very controversial. Before the 2013 Act judges had stated that for them to hold that a hearing in which the party affected is not told what is alleged against him 'negates the judicial function' and damages 'the integrity of the judicial process': *AF v Home Secretary* [2009] UKHL 28 at [84] and *Al Rawi* at [83]. Zuckerman, §19.92, described closed procedures as 'the antithesis of due process'.

It is striking that CPR Part 82.2 provides that the overriding objective of enabling the court to deal with a case justly must be given effect to so as to ensure that information is not disclosed in a way which will be damaging to national security. Lord Lloyd-Jones has described the balance Parliament struck in the 2013 Act between the interests of national security and justice as 'an attempt to balance competing interests which are, ultimately, irreconcilable': *Belhaj v DPP* [2018] UKSC 33 at [41]. But the courts recognise that 'save maybe in an extreme case' they 'are obliged to apply the law … as laid down in statute by Parliament': *Bank Mellat v HM Treasury (No 1)* [2013] UKSC 38 at [8]. They also appear to regard the statutory conditions, particularly the express provision to secure compliance with ECHR Article 6, as appropriate safeguards: *R (Sarkandi) v Foreign Secretary* [2015] EWCA Civ 687 at [58] and *Belhaj* at [14] and [41]–[42].

The position taken by the Strasbourg court, summarised above, may mean that there will be no difference between that court and United Kingdom courts. But the deficiencies of the special advocate system highlighted by evidence from special advocates led the Joint Committee on Human Rights to conclude in its 19th Report in 2006–07 that it was hard not to describe the system as 'Kafkaesque' or like the Star Chamber. The Committee considered that closed hearings and the special advocate system are not only offensive to the basic principles of justice in which lawyers are steeped, but also 'very much against the basic principles of fair play as the lay public would understand them'. The system also removes the element of democratic accountability which open justice provides. From the point of view of the excluded parties, the principal defect is that special advocates cannot take instructions from them on closed material so the scope for challenging that material is limited. As Lord Kerr stated in *Al Rawi* at [93]–[94] 'evidence which has been insulated from challenge may positively mislead' and the process is 'a distinctly second-best attempt to secure a just outcome'.

# 7

## An Independent and Impartial Judiciary

> An independent, impartial, honest and competent judiciary is
> integral to upholding the rule of law, engendering public confidence
> and dispensing justice.

Latimer House Principles, IV

This articulation of the principles of judicial independence and impartiality was endorsed by the Commonwealth Heads of Government in 2003. The many other international agreements doing so include the UN General Assembly's 1948 Universal Declaration of Human Rights, article 10, its 1985 'Basic Principles', ECHR article 6 in 1950, and the 2002 Bangalore Principles of Judicial Conduct endorsed by the UN Human Rights Commission in 2003. Despite this wide recognition, the principle has faced challenges in many countries recently. For example, in Poland, since 2015, legislation has sought to put the National Council of the Judiciary, formerly an independent body, under the control of the legislature. In Bulgaria, there is a large political quota on the Supreme Judicial Council. There are concerns about the impact of a 2020 Hong Kong national security law on civil liberties and the power of the government to select the judges who are to hear cases brought under it.

This chapter is about the judiciary of England and Wales, but the position is broadly similar in Scotland and Northern Ireland. It considers why judicial independence is fundamental to the rule of law, how the accountability of the judiciary is secured in a way consistent with that independence, and the principal external and internal challenges to it.

The need to engender public confidence in the judiciary also means that it is important to have a judiciary which is a fair reflection of society. In recent years progress has been made with gender and ethnic diversity, particularly in appointments to the district and circuit benches and tribunals, but less so for the senior judiciary, especially with regard to ethnic diversity: Shetreet and Turenne, §4.20 ff.

In England and Wales, the constitutional origin of judicial independence is the Act of Settlement 1701 which gave senior judges security of tenure 'during good behaviour'. Until 2005 there was, however, no express statutory reference to the principle as such. That has now been provided by the 'guarantee of continued judicial independence' in section 3 of the CRA 2005. Leaving aside what, if any, significance the word 'continued' has, what do judicial independence and impartiality mean and why are they integral to upholding the rule of law?

# I. LESSONS FROM HISTORY

Some of the answers to both questions are revealed by sketching the position before 1701 when the judiciary was not independent. Judges were servants of the crown and an integral part of the governance of England, performing many administrative duties as what we would call civil servants as well as hearing and deciding disputes. They were generally removable at the pleasure of the Crown and their appointments ceased on the death of the reigning monarch. They were not financially secure and were often paid irregularly: one fourteenth-century Chief Justice, Roger of Brabazon, was paid on only four occasions between 1294 and 1306. The consequence was that judges had to supplement their income from other sources, including fees from litigants, the sale of offices, and even bribery.

In the constitutionally turbulent period before the outbreak of the English Civil War in 1642, judges were subjected to pressure by James I and Charles I. The sanction for those who refused to comply with government, that is royal, policy could be dismissal or suspension. An early indication was the dismissal in 1616 of Coke CJ, reputed to be the greatest lawyer of the age, after he refused to say that he would stop a case if ordered to by the king. Additionally, the struggle between the Crown and Parliament meant that both sides sought to exert pressure on the judges who had to determine the respective boundaries of royal and Parliamentary power. While the king had the power of dismissal, and control over judges' remuneration and promotion, Parliament had other means, notably the power of impeachment and Parliamentary inquiries into decisions in individual cases, particularly constitutional cases. A notable example is that, after the *Case of Ship-Money, R v Hampden* (1637) 3 St Tr 825, held that the king had indirect power to impose tax as an incident to the exercise of his prerogative power, the House of Commons sought to impeach the judges in the case.

Improper interference with judges continued after the restoration of the monarchy in 1660. Charles II introduced forced retirement to remove judges for political reasons, sacking 11 in as many years. James II dismissed 12 judges without pensions in four years, mostly for refusing to recognise his claim to dispense with statutes: Baker, 179. Because judicial office was less secure, the overall quality of the judiciary declined, the judges who survived were mistrusted by the public, and the quality of justice was at risk. This was because, in the words of Lord Bingham, judges 'must be independent of anybody or anything which might lead them to decide issues coming before them on anything other than the legal and factual merits of the case as, in the exercise of their own judgment, they consider them to be': Bingham 2011, 92.

The Act of Settlement changed the constitutional position. As well as security of tenure for senior judges (until 1760 only until the death of the monarch), it provided that 'upon the address of both houses of Parliament it may be lawful to remove them'. It also provided that their salaries be 'ascertained and established', although that was not done until 1760. By 1830 the annual salary of a High Court judge was £5,000, the equivalent of about £340,000 today. In 2019, it was £188,901, more than judges in most European countries and United States Federal judges, and in itself more than adequate to preserve independence.

Because the most successful practitioners from whom appointments have traditionally been made earn significantly more, for many years some have considered that there is a risk that, if the ablest candidates cannot be attracted, the standing and reputation of the judiciary might be lowered: see for example Bingham 2000, 66. They see a subtle link between independence and remuneration because of a perceived relationship between what someone earns and that person's status. There is some force in this but, although some very suitable high-fliers may decline appointment because of the salary, others do so because they enjoy legal practice or because other features of being a judge do not attract them. Recent difficulties of recruitment have resulted from a combination of the impact of a heavier workload, less attractive working conditions and, since 2011, detrimental changes to the pension entitlements of younger judges. The pensions problem led to the introduction in 2019 of a substantial 'recruitment and retention allowance'.

Politics continued to affect appointments until the early part of the twentieth century. Before the appointment of Lord Goddard as Lord Chief Justice in 1946 it had been the practice to give first refusal to government law officers. Between 1714 and 1760 two-thirds of judges had been MPs and between 1885 and 1905 Lord Halsbury made a number of appointments which were widely criticised as showing party bias: Baker, 179; Stevens 1978, 84–85. It was not until after his tenure that appointments began to be made on the basis of 'high legal and professional qualification' rather than political affiliations: Haldane 253; Stevens 1978, 191. Before the reforms in the office of Lord Chancellor, whose role in each of the three branches of the state is summarised at 11, he had the decisive role in making appointments, although the Lord Chief Justice and other senior judges in leadership positions were extensively consulted.

## II. INDIVIDUAL INDEPENDENCE

Our history shows that judicial independence is necessary so that laws are enforced free from the influence of external vested interests, whether governmental or other. Today those other interests may include pressure groups, business, the media, and litigants. Judicial independence, security of tenure, and financial security remove the risk of political and other interference in individual cases, and of corruption. These reasons show the importance of individual independence in the sense used by Lord Bingham in the passage quoted at 99. Such adjudicative independence in an individual judge's decision-making is firmly established and generally clearly understood. It is now embodied in section 3(5) of the CRA which provides that 'the Lord Chancellor and other Ministers of the Crown must not seek to influence particular judicial decisions through any special access to the judiciary'.

As to tenure, before 1959, senior judges had lifetime tenure during good behaviour. This ensured continuity and experience but took no account of a decline in the abilities of a judge as a result of old age or ill health. The risk of such decline increases with age but, while there has been a means of in effect removing a senior judge who is 'disabled by permanent infirmity from performing the duties of the office' since 1973 (see now Senior Courts Act 1981, section 11(8) and (9)) there was no means of doing so for lesser disability. Accordingly, the introduction of retirement age for newly appointed senior judges, at first of 75 and from 1993 of 70 for all judges, was not in any way inconsistent with judicial independence. It was perceived as a way of maintaining public confidence in the judiciary by reducing the risk of those with reduced faculties continuing to serve when they could no longer properly carry out their duties. But in 2021 a number of factors, including the increase in unfilled vacancies in the High Court and in the number of early retirements in that court and the Court of Appeal, and increased longevity led to a decision to raise the retirement age to 75. Given the numbers of early retirements, increasing the age of retirement may not in the long term be entirely effective in addressing the recruitment problem. Consideration also needs to be given to how, given security of tenure if of good behaviour, to handle a person who is still capable of doing the work, but not at the pace they achieved when younger.

Another relevant aspect of tenure concerns the fact that continuity and stability are important components in underpinning the independence of the judiciary. It is therefore desirable that those appointed to the High Court or to leadership posts should be able to serve for a minimum number of years before reaching the retirement age. They gain experience and, in the case of High Court judges, provide a pool of suitably qualified judges available for selection for promotion. While it was unfortunate that excellent candidates were precluded from applying to be Lord Chief Justice in 2017, the requirement that the person appointed should be able to serve a minimum of four years was, when seen in this light, correct. Of the 18 Lord Chief Justices since 1874, on appointment 12 were aged 64 or under. All but four of those appointed since 1940 served for five years or more. Of those who did not, two vacated the office only because they were appointed to preside in cases in the UK's final court of appeal and one vacated the office after being diagnosed with a terminal illness. Only one was appointed less than five years before his statutory retirement age.

For similar reasons, the proposal in the Prison and Courts Bill 2017 that it should be possible to appoint the Lord Chief Justice and Heads of Division on a fixed-term basis, was misconceived. The effect would have been to make the office more like that of a revolving chair of a committee with a real risk that it would be diminished. Members of the legislative and executive branches of government, and other judges who do not favour the initiatives of the current office holder would be able to seek to delay them in the hope that the next holder of the office had a different view. A regular revolving door might also lead to increased jostling for position and opportunities for currying favour.

The importance of individual independence is also reflected in the longstanding absolute immunity of senior judges from civil liability for what they say or do in the exercise of their judicial function, even where malice is alleged: *Hamond v Howell* (1677) 2 Mod 218; *Sirros v Moore* [1975] QB 118. The immunity has been justified as being for the benefit of the public rather than to protect a malicious or corrupt judge. In *Re MC (A minor)* [1985] AC 528, 541 it was said that if

> one judge in a thousand acts dishonestly … to the detriment of a party before him, it is less harmful to the health of society to leave that party without a remedy than that the nine hundred and ninety nine honest judges should be harassed by vexatious litigation alleging malice …

In some respects, the immunity is too wide and in others too narrow. The prime example of excessive narrowness is that county court and tribunal judges and magistrates are generally not immune for acts outside their jurisdiction. Making the scope of the immunity depend on the level of post held seems irrational. But the attempt in *Sirros v Moore* at 136 to remove it and give immunity for all judicial acts done in the honest belief that they are within jurisdiction failed. It was considered that so funda-mental a change would require legislation: *Re MC (A minor)* at 550. In the case of lay magistrates this was done in 1997: see now Courts Act 2003, section 32.

The prime example of excessive width is immunity even where a claimant demonstrates an arguable case of malice, personal animus or corruption by a judge. That sits very poorly with rule of law values: Olowofoyeku, 64; Shetreet and Turenne §7.5. The fear of litigation can undoubtedly distort judgement and produce defensive professional practices. But it has not led to absolute immunity for other professionals such as solicitors, surgeons and physicians. One might question why a filter such as those discussed at 78 in relation to access to courts by vexatious litigants and mental patients would be inconsistent with judicial independence.

There are of course other means of redress for judicial misbehaviour, in particular the ability to appeal and the complaint and disciplinary system. Sedley 2015, 279, has said the disciplinary system, now in statutory regulations, 'is a necessary part of the rule of law'. Those, together with the criminal prosecution of a judge who has acted corruptly by taking bribes or perverting the course of justice, probably provide adequate accountability for rule of law purposes.

# III. INSTITUTIONAL INDEPENDENCE

Our history also shows that interference with individual judges has an impact on the authority and public confidence in, and support for, the judiciary as a whole. The highly critical reactions to controversial or sensitive modern decisions and the abuse of the judges deciding them by attacking their integrity or patriotism have a similar impact. Both suggest that, as well as individual independence, it is important for the judiciary to have a degree of institutional or collective independence from the other branches of the state and that the line between individual and institutional independence can be a fine one.

The principles are excellently captured in the Supreme Court of Canada's much cited statement in *Valente v The Queen* [1985] 2 SCR 673 at [15] that

> the traditional constitutional value of judicial independence … connotes not merely a state of mind or attitude in the actual exercise of judicial functions, but a status or relationship to others, particularly to the executive branch of government, that rests on objective conditions or guarantees.

What is required is judicial control over the administrative decisions that bear directly and immediately on the exercise of the judicial function: *Valente* at [52]. The degree of institutional independence differs in different states, but the Consultative Council of European Judges has stated that it generally involves independence from the legislature and the executive in appointments, promotion, career development, training and discipline, and court administration; and protection of the image of justice.

In the UK, until the CRA 2005, however, because the Lord Chancellor and Lord Advocate, senior government ministers, were heads of the judiciary in England and Wales and Scotland, there was 'little independence in a collective, or institutional, sense' from the executive: Woodhouse, 122. Matters such as deployment, although formally the responsibility of the Lord Chancellor, were, however, in practice delegated to the Heads of Division of the High Court and the Senior Presiding Judge.

The idea of institutional independence is controversial. Some iterations of it treat the judiciary as a separate arm of government, independent of the legislature and the executive branches, with the judiciary running the court system, subject only to funds voted by Parliament: see Lord Browne-Wilkinson 1988. There are, however, many pressing claims on finite national resources. Our system of democracy gives the power of deciding how public money is to be spent to Parliament and the executive in tandem, and not to the judiciary: see Lord Mustill in *R v Home Secretary, ex p, Fire Brigades Union* [1995] 2 AC 513, 567. But the absence of institutional independence has in the past meant that 'management concepts quite inappropriate to the unique function of administering justice have been allowed to intrude': Bingham 2000, 66–67. One example is the view referred to at 77, that, unlike health and defence, civil justice is not a public good to be provided by government but a service to be paid for by its users.

The position was changed by the CRA 2005 which significantly altered the nature of the office of Lord Chancellor and created a Judicial Appointments Commission and a UK Supreme Court. The Act thus largely replaced an important area of the unwritten constitution with a new legislative scheme. The Lord Chief Justice became the head of the judiciary of England and Wales. The responsibilities of the office are to represent the views of the judiciary to Parliament, the Lord Chancellor and ministers generally; to make arrangements for welfare, training and guidance within the resources made available by government; and to make arrangements for the deployment of judges and the allocation of work within the courts: CRA section 7. Responsibility for complaints against judges and the disciplinary system is shared with the Lord Chancellor: CRA sections 108–18.

As previously noted, judicial independence as an overarching constitutional principle in the United Kingdom sits very uneasily with Parliamentary sovereignty. Despite its name and the references to 'continued judicial independence', the CRA does not in itself provide an answer to what Stevens 2002 at 96 describes as 'apparently irreconcilable concepts'. It does, however, provide some statutory authority for institutional independence in the 'guarantee of continued judicial independence' in section 3.

Section 3(1) provides that all government ministers and 'all with responsibility for matters relating to the judiciary or otherwise to the administration of justice must uphold the continued independence of the judiciary'. The fact that it is not explicitly confined to individual independence in the way that section 3(5) is (see 109), suggests that notwithstanding the absence of an express reference, section 3(1) encompasses a degree of institutional independence. The duty applies to prosecuting authorities, the police, and the legislature, including Parliamentary Committees considering these matters and increasingly taking evidence from judges. It also applies to judges holding leadership positions, requiring them in their dealings with other judges to maintain an appropriate degree of internal independence: see for example *Findlay v UK* (1997) 24 EHRR 221 at [75]–[77]. They must ensure that the individual independence of each judge is maintained, in particular their right to decide cases entirely freely and independently. Judges must accept some proactive court management in order to achieve an efficient and effective system but, as a recent Lord Chief Justice stated, leadership judges must ensure that the system of judicial governance 'can never be used to stifle or inhibit the expression in judgments of views that might not appeal to the mainstream of judicial opinion': Thomas 2017A, §138.

A clear demonstration of the recognition of a degree of institutional independence, albeit filtered through the Lord Chancellor, is seen in the three factors in section 3(6)(a)–(c) that the Lord Chancellor 'must have regard to'. Bearing in mind that the holder of this office is also the Secretary of State for Justice, with the potential conflicts referred to at 74–75, it is the Lord Chancellor's responsibility to secure funding for courts and tribunals and their judges, and it is that person who is accountable to Parliament for the administration of justice and expenditure.

The first factor, 'the need to defend that independence', largely duplicates the duty in section 3(1) to uphold it but appears to go further by requiring active defence against conduct of third parties which threatens judicial independence. The examples at 110–111, however, show that Lord Chancellors have not always given such defence and that it is vital for there to be a better understanding of what is required. The second factor, 'the need for the judiciary to have the support necessary to enable them to exercise their functions', is primarily concerned with the institution rather than individual judges. It supplements the Lord Chancellor's statutory duty to ensure that there is an efficient and effective system to support the carrying on of the business of the courts and tribunals, discussed at 74. The third factor, 'the need for the public interest in matters relating to the judiciary and the administration of justice to be properly represented in decisions affecting those matters', is also concerned with the institution.

As to appointments in England and Wales, the Judicial Appointments Commission is composed of a lay chair, five lay members, seven judges at different levels, including one lay magistrate, and two legal professionals. Appointments must be 'solely on merit', although where two persons are of equal merit, the selection body may prefer one over the other 'for the purpose of increasing diversity': CRA, section 63.

The creation of the Commission has largely removed the Lord Chancellor from the decision-making process for High Court and Court of Appeal appointments and, since the Crime and Courts Act 2013, eliminated it for other appointments. There are similar bodies for Scotland and Northern Ireland. It has been said, in a somewhat critical tone, that there are 'high levels of influence by senior judges' on appointments: Gee, Hazell, Malleson and O'Brien, 159 and 179. Although there are dangers in a process of self-replication, that influence may reflect more institutional independence from government, which is not necessarily a matter for criticism.

Since the enactment of the CRA in 2005, changes in the administrative and managerial responsibilities of selected members of the senior judiciary reflect the recognition of institutional independence. In 2008 the Lord Chief Justice and the Lord Chancellor agreed that, in the light of the creation of the Ministry of Justice in 2007, they should have dual leadership over what is now the Courts and Tribunals Service. That agreement is recorded in what is known as the Framework Document which requires the Courts and Tribunals Service to be accountable to both of them. As well as formally taking on responsibility for matters such as deployment, previously undertaken as the Lord Chancellor's delegate, the judiciary was to have a 'partnership' with government in the administration of the Courts and Tribunals Service. Judges now serve on its board and have an explicit role in strategic planning and decision-making.

The new arrangements have required the judiciary to step outside their core function of deciding cases more often and to develop their governance structure and a different relationship with the other branches of the State: Thomas 2017B §4. To assist them in their administrative functions, there is now a Judicial Executive Board supported by a substantially staffed Judicial Office. There are sections responsible for Communications, Media Support, Human Resources, Complaints, as well as private offices to support the Lord Chief Justice, the Heads of Division and the Senior Presiding Judge.

The significant administrative and managerial functions of the judiciary, and the revived active role in promoting reform to the administration of justice, bring challenges discussed at 113–114. It is important that they do not turn the judiciary into just another 'player' in the policy and political process. That will undoubtedly require the development of new constitutional conventions.

# IV. ACCOUNTABILITY

The judiciary recognised from the outset that greater independence and administrative and managerial responsibilities would lead to calls for greater accountability. This is an admirable concept, but its breadth requires further explanation. In 2007, the Judicial Executive Board and the Judges' Council approved a document which made a distinction between 'explanatory' accountability and 'sacrificial' accountability. Explanatory accountability occurs in judgments which give the reasons for decisions in individual cases and by the increased live streaming of hearings in selected cases. Such accountability also occurs where judges in leadership positions, particularly the Lord Chief Justice, report on the administration of justice in reports, in public evidence to Parliamentary Committees, and in lectures and speeches. This is regarded as consistent with judicial independence and may indeed enhance it.

'Sacrificial' accountability involves losing your job. In the absence of safeguards such as those in the Act of Settlement, and the procedures dealing with discipline and ill-health referred to at 101 and 104, sacrificial accountability is seen as inconsistent with independence. Accordingly, not all forms of accountability are consistent with independence, and one cannot simply say that accountability is the *quid pro quo* for independence. How then can a system secure accountability in ways consistent with independence?

For an individual judge, accountability is primarily through the appeal process and the statutory arrangements governing discipline and removal for misconduct or disability. The outcomes of appeals are published with full reasons, which, where the appeal is allowed, point out the judge's errors. This provides ample opportunity for comment by the media and the wider public. The comments can be highly critical, particularly in high profile cases on sensitive subjects including sentencing for serious crimes and immigration decisions. This is legitimate in a democracy, provided that the constraints within which a judge must operate in order to apply the law are not simply ignored by the critics, and the criticism is not simply abusive, as it sometimes is, see 110. This limitation is necessary because abuse can be corrosive of public confidence in the judiciary, the justice system, and the rule of law in a similar way to the way cries of 'fake news' may affect public confidence in the media.

Institutional accountability is something which, like governance, has evolved since the CRA 2005 largely as a result of initiatives by the judiciary. They have recognised the value of communications aimed at increasing the understanding of the public and the other parts of the state of the role of judges, and the developments and pressures in the court system. Those holding the office of Lord Chief Justice have increasingly given evidence to Parliamentary Committees. They also hold an annual press conference to seek to increase understanding of the courts and the justice system and, since 2012 have published and presented a Report to Parliament annually.

Published guidance by the Judicial Executive Board deals with the circumstances in which judges can appropriately give evidence to Parliamentary Committees and about engagement with the executive on legislative proposals and draft bills. It states that constitutional convention and the need to preserve independence mean that engagement should be limited to technical and procedural aspects of proposals. It is, however, permissible for the Lord Chief Justice or a relevant leadership judge to comment on the merits of a policy where that policy affects judicial independence or the rule of law.

## V. EXTERNAL AND INTERNAL CHALLENGES AND OPPORTUNITIES

External pressure whether by government, the media, or interest groups may potentially challenge both individual and institutional judicial independence. It is most likely to occur in high-profile cases concerning sentencing, immigration and terrorism. It is also likely when serving judges step outside their core function of deciding cases, for example by chairing inquiries.

The need for adjudicative independence from government in an individual judge's decision-making is generally well understood. CRA section 3(5) safeguards it by prohibiting government ministers from seeking 'to influence particular judicial decisions through any special access to the judiciary'. There are, however, occasions when things go wrong. One example is where a governmental party to litigation seeks to prevent the judges hearing a case from seeing material filed in the proceedings. This happened in *Privacy International v Foreign Secretary & others* [2020] UKIPTrib IPT 17 86 CH where the Secret Intelligence Service, MI6, asked the Secretary of the Investigatory Powers Tribunal not to pass reports provided to the Tribunal by the Investigatory Powers Commissioner to the judges hearing the case. The request was refused. Those representing government and the security services apologised and accepted that something had gone seriously wrong.

It is also inappropriate for the judges involved to discuss the way the government might achieve its policy aims lawfully after it has lost a case. A notable example arose after *A v Home Secretary* [2004] UKHL 56 decided that detention without trial of non-British citizens under the Antiterrorism, Crime and Security Act 2001 was incompatible with the ECHR. The then Home Secretary wished to meet the judges who decided the case to discuss how those suspected of being terrorists could effectively be dealt with without such incompatibility. He was exasperated by their unwillingness to do so: Evidence to HL Constitution Committee 2006–07, Q 123. It may be that he had not thought through the implications of discussing a particular policy which would almost inevitably be later contested in the courts with the very judges who had previously ruled against the government when considering a policy designed to deal with precisely the same problem.

A final example, less tied to a particular case, is a letter that Home Office officials sent to the President of the Immigration and Asylum Chamber of the First tier Tribunal during the COVID-19 lockdown in April 2020. It expressed surprise at the number of applications for bail by those in immigration detention that succeeded and asked for written reasons for granting bail to be given in addition to the oral reasons given at the hearing. The President robustly rejected the request, stating that the independent judiciary decided bail applications in accordance with the law and guidance: Free Movement blog and *The Guardian* 6 May 2020.

In the case of comment by the media and other individuals and groups, there must be a balance between the need to protect the judicial process against distortion and illegitimate pressure, and the interests of open discussion of matters of public interest in public life including controversial or sensitive decisions, and a free press: Consultative Council of European Judges 2007, §63, approved by the Venice Commission 2010, §58. But the tone of some comments shows that the line referred to between legitimate robust criticism and abuse is not always observed. The reactions to the decision of the Divisional Court in *Miller 1* [2016] EWHC 2768 (Admin) that it was necessary for there to be legislation before the UK served notice under Article 50 of its intention to leave the EU included a newspaper headline describing the judges as 'enemies of the people' who 'defied 17.4m Brexit voters'. In cases such as that, and *Miller 2 & Cherry*, the challenge to the prorogation of Parliament discussed at 13 and 125, the judges have found themselves standing between the executive government and Parliament and in a similar position to the one they were in in the period before the outbreak of the English Civil War.

There is a difference between challenging the content of a judgment and attacking the character and integrity of the judges handing down that judgment. Abusive attacks on individual judges have an impact on public confidence in the judiciary and on their authority. When there are such attacks, the Lord Chancellor must take a proactive stance in defending them publicly. Unfortunately, this has not always happened. Some of the starkest examples were the reactions to a case in 2006 where a man who abducted and sexually assaulted a three-year old girl was sentenced to life imprisonment with a minimum term which complied with the applicable sentencing guidelines, and to the Divisional Court's 2016 decision in *Miller 1*.

In the 2006 case, although the minimum term complied with the applicable guidelines, the Home Secretary criticised it as unduly lenient and not reflecting the seriousness of the crime. Other politicians including Lord Falconer QC, then Lord Chancellor, defended the Home Secretary's right to say the sentence was too low because he had not attacked the sentencing judge. The press was less restrained. Their comments included 'the arrogance of judges in their mink-lined ivory towers who leave the rest of us to cope with the real crisis of soaring crime'; the judiciary is 'deluded, out-of-touch and frankly deranged'; and 'combining arrogance with downright wickedness': for a full account see HL Constitution Committee 2006–07, §§45–49 and 2017B §57. The

Committee concluded that it was clear that there had been 'a systemic failure' in the relationship between the Lord Chancellor and the judiciary. Lord Falconer had not fulfilled his duty in a satisfactory manner. The Committee also stated that the senior judiciary 'could have acted more quickly to head off the inflammatory and unfair press coverage'.

The reaction of Liz Truss MP, then Lord Chancellor, to the media coverage of the Divisional Court's decision in *Miller 1* was to state that she was a huge supporter of the independence of the judiciary but that her strong belief in a free press meant that it would be wrong for her as a government minister to condemn what the press had written.

In both these cases some of the newspapers' attacks went beyond the strong criticism of the decisions, which is legitimate, and amounted to an abuse of the individual judges and the judiciary as an institution which required 'defending'. It is difficult to see how on either occasion the Lord Chancellor fulfilled the statutory requirement to 'uphold the continuing independence of the judiciary' in CRA section 3(1) or to have regard to 'the need to defend' that independence in section 3(6)(a).

What happened also shows that there is no common understanding of what our constitutional framework requires and raises the question of whether the statutory requirements are aspirational rather than enforceable. In principle, the meaning of statutory language is justiciable, but it is doubtful whether section 3 could form the basis of a direct challenge to a failure by the Lord Chancellor in relation to a concept as multi-faceted as judicial independence. Leaving aside any legal duty under sections 3(1) and 3(6), since the basis of a constitutional convention is that those subject to it believe they are bound by it, it is difficult to see that one exists in relation to what the Lord Chancellor and other ministers are required to do in circumstances such as these. Who then is to 'uphold' and 'defend' judicial independence? Senior judges have an interest in the question which makes it undesirable that it should be them.

Another potential external challenge arises as a result of the government's use of serving judges to chair public inquiries, particularly those with a strong political flavour or involving broad issues of social or economic policy. These show how, when judges step outside their core function of deciding cases, their independence and impartiality is more likely to be challenged. Even inquiries into accidents and deaths may involve consideration of broad areas of policy because the underlying public disquiet may concern such policies. Notable examples are the Scarman Inquiry into riots in Brixton in 1981 and the Macpherson Inquiry into the police's investigation of the murder of a black teenager in 1993, where the underlying concern was racism in the Metropolitan Police.

Of the notable inquiries set up since 1990, almost two-thirds have been chaired by a serving or retired judge. The fundamental reason for using judges is that they are independent and impartial but using them is potentially dangerous to that independence: see further Beatson 2005. Appointing a judge does not depoliticise an inherently political issue. Because the report is not subject to appeal and not binding, those disagreeing with it may seek to discredit its findings by criticising the judge. Secondly, it is the government which determines the terms of reference of the inquiry, chooses the person to conduct it and has a large say in the procedure to be used. Thirdly, there has been increasing recourse to judicial review to challenge procedural decisions during an inquiry. There were four successful judicial reviews of the Saville inquiry into the deaths of Irish republicans shot by British paratroopers in 1972.

After the report, if the government or a public body involved is criticised, the judge risks being described as naïve and unfamiliar with the reality of government. Similarly, the procedure used may be described as unfair, as happened to the 1996 report by Sir Richard Scott on 'the Arms for Iraq affair'. If the government is cleared, the judge will be described as an establishment lackey, as happened to Lord Hutton after his 2004 report concluded that an allegation that Downing Street probably knew that a statement that Iraq could deploy its biological and chemical weapons within 45 minutes was unfounded. Such criticism may mean the report does not bring the matter to an end. Lord Hutton's inquiry did not do so. Two days after he reported, the government set up a new inquiry chaired by a former Secretary to the Cabinet to examine the intelligence evidence that led the UK into the war.

There are also internal challenges to judicial independence. These may arise from the forceful personality of one of the judges hearing a case. For example, Lord Diplock is said to have discouraged separate concurring judgments. Lord Wilberforce described Lord Diplock as possessing 'the quality of persuading his colleagues to the extreme' and Sir Stephen Sedley and Godfrey le Quesne QC that 'the disdain he found increasingly difficult to conceal for judicial views contrary to his own sometimes stifled discussion and dissent': quoted by Heydon, 216–17.

Other internal challenges arise because of the significant administrative and managerial functions of judges in leadership positions and the governance structure they have developed. One sensitive area is the allocation of work. It is clearly desirable to allocate work according to a judge's expertise but taking account of the position taken by a particular judge on a controversial issue in decisions within that area of expertise is not legitimate: see 105.

The *Guide to Judicial Conduct* provides that leadership judges 'will treat everyone equally' and that when involved in selecting for appointment, promotion or specific roles they will make decisions by reference to 'sound, objective criteria', on the basis of 'personal merit, experience, competence, performance, skills, and abilities'. As to training, appraisal and deployment it states they 'will act so as to provide equality of opportunity and treatment'. This will not be provided if the member of a court with the greatest expertise in an area is allocated all the significant cases in that area in a first instance court, or where a small cadre of judges is selected to do all the work in a new area, without others being given the opportunity to express interest. One consequence may be that when there is a need for a person with that expertise in a higher court there is only one plausible candidate. Deployment which is likely to lead to this is not compatible with the fundamental values and principles that underpin judicial independence.

The revival of activism by the judiciary in using its knowledge of the court system to improve it by initiating and leading reform to its administration and delivery of justice such as online dispute resolution and the provision of technical and procedural advice to government also has implications for independence: see Briggs, chapter 6 and Thomas 2017A, §53ff. Although similar activities have been undertaken in the past, the judicial initiatives and assistance then were within a constitutional framework with much less separation of powers and in which the Lord Chancellor was head of the judiciary.

If the judiciary as an institution is proactive in devising and promoting a reform and in advising on policy there is a risk of it being drawn into political controversy about aspects of the administration of justice, or any rate of being seen as just another lobbying group seeking to advance its own interests. Close identification with a programme of reform, even one directly concerned with the administration of justice, and actively promoting it in partnership with government, may jeopardise the perception that the judiciary is institutionally independent of government, particularly where government has not provided adequate funding for the reform.

For issues directly concerned with the administration of the court system, however, the alternative would leave problem solving to those with less knowledge of the court system and perhaps less concern with the values and principles needed for continued judicial independence. So, while sensitive handling is needed, the active roles of the judiciary in promoting the court reform programme, and of Sir Rupert Jackson in promoting the implementation of his 2009 review of civil litigation costs by preparing draft rules for the Rules Committee and delivering 'implementation lectures' are probably unavoidable.

The position is different where an inquiry is not directly concerned with the administration of justice and the judiciary does not have an institutional view about the need for reform. Sir Scott Baker and Sir Brian Leveson were unwilling to be drawn into any discussion of the merits of the proposals in their 2011 and 2012 reports respectively reviewing the Extradition Act 2003 and the culture, practices and ethics of the British Press. There are good reasons for that approach, which is analogous to judges not getting drawn into public discussion about judgments they have given: see HL Committee on the Inquiries Act 2005 §268. Firstly, the judge might be drawn into giving an opinion on a variation on a recommendation without hearing the evidence. Secondly, the judge might be drawn into political debate with the accompanying risks to the perception of impartiality. Thirdly, the implementation of reform proposals is the shared responsibility and domain of the legislative and executive branches of the state rather than the judiciary. Despite the difference of context, these reasons also have some relevance to proposals on which the judiciary has an institutional view.

If reform led by a single judge or on which a particular judge has advised government is implemented, should the judge who led it or provided the advice hear a case concerning the reform? Might a reasonable person legitimately see the judge leading the reform or the judiciary advocating it as not impartial in relation to disputes about it, or is there no real problem? What if the reform is one that was the result of a Judicial Executive Board initiative or, as in the case of the review of civil litigation costs, has been endorsed by that body? The fact that a judge has taken a view on an issue in a previous case which has been overruled does not in itself preclude him or her sitting on a later case on the same point. This is because precedent must and will be followed. Again, views expressed by judges in a book or an article do not preclude them from sitting. The judge should have an open mind because the views previously expressed have not been tested on the forensic anvil of adversarial argument in court. But the importance of perception may mean that it would be prudent in the case of a judge-led reform for others to hear the early cases on a point, particularly if the judge responsible for the report has responded robustly to criticisms of it.

# 8

# The Separation of Powers and the Balance of Responsibilities

This chapter considers the way the separation of powers is reflected in our constitutional arrangements, whether such separation is fostered by a category of statutes recognised as 'constitutional', and the balance of responsibilities between courts and other branches of the state.

## I. THE SEPARATION OF POWERS

Classically the three locations of constitutional powers and functions are those of the legislative, the executive, and the judicial branches of the state. Sir Stephen Sedley 2015, 190, considers that today three further locations could be added, namely the established church, the media, and the security and intelligence services. While there is some force in his view that each 'possesses a sufficient measure of autonomy to rank to some degree as a discrete element in the governance of the state', this book only considers the three classical locations.

What some have described as the pure or fundamental form of the principle requires an *a priori* classification of powers as either legislative, executive or judicial to determine which institution of the state should exercise a given function completely independently of the others. But as Sedley 2015, 172, stated:

> Plainly this is unreal: the judiciary has to be appointed and paid by a body other than itself; the law it interprets and applies has to be made in substantial part by a legislature; the legislature is largely dependent for its own functioning on the executive and political heads …; the executive requires a parliamentary mandate for much of what it does; and the courts have to be able to say whether the executive is acting within its mandate.

France and the United States of America have been the states with forms of government closest to the pure form of the separation of powers. Until 1958, in France ministers could not sit in the legislature and the ordinary courts did not determine whether the legislature was acting constitutionally or whether the acts and omissions of the executive were lawful. Until the creation of the Conseil Constitutionnel, the Constitutional Council, in that year, the legislature itself determined whether it was acting constitutionally. The Conseil d'État, the Administrative Council, still determines the legality of executive action. The United States constitution seeks to avoid concentrations of power by forbidding those who hold executive office from being members of the legislature and vice versa, but it is the federal courts which have the ability to determine whether legislative and executive acts are legal and thus to restrain their exercises of power. In many other democracies with balanced constitutions, however, government ministers with executive responsibility are also members of the legislature and accountable to it, as well as to the electorate and to the ordinary courts.

As stated at 5–6, the rationale for a principle of the separation of powers is to have a system of checks and balances between different branches of the state which restrains tyranny and the abuse of power. Those who make or who administer the law should not determine whether an individual has broken that law. The threefold division of labour, between a legislator, an administrative official and an independent judge has been said to be a 'necessary condition for the rule of law in a modern society': Henderson, 5. This is because 'for the administrator to act within the boundaries set by the laws, there must be some other person with final authority to determine what the laws mean, and to do so by a method different from the administrative one. This official is the judge': see Unger, 177.

It has therefore been said that, as a general rule 'under our constitution and subject to the sovereign power of Parliament it is the function of the courts and not of political bodies to resolve legal questions': *A v Home Secretary* [2004] UKHL 445 at [29]. There are many other statements to the same effect. For instance, in *Duport Steels Ltd v Sirs* [1980] 1 WLR 142, 157 Lord Diplock stated that the British constitution 'is firmly based on the separation of powers; Parliament makes the laws, the judiciary interpret them'. More recently, in *R (Privacy International) v Investigatory Powers Tribunal* [2019] UKSC 22 at [160] Lord Carnwath stated that 'it is a necessary corollary of the sovereignty of Parliament that there should exist an authoritative and independent body which can interpret and mediate legislation made by Parliament'.

One reason for such separation is to ensure that ministers and public authorities do not make errors which extend the area over which the legislature has granted them jurisdiction. Since *Anisminic v Foreign Compensation Commission* [1969] 2 AC 69, discussed at 44 and 144, this has enabled courts to substitute their conclusions for those of the public authority on all questions of law. It is, however, important to emphasise, as will be seen at 129–130, that they may be reluctant to do so where the statutory language, although legally having only one meaning, is very imprecise, and they will be unwilling to do so if it involves a policy matter which is more appropriately decided by the democratically elected organs of the state. Such issues are ones for Parliament and legislation or for the executive branch of government rather than for the courts.

Another aspect of separation is that it is a basic principle of our constitution and a component of the rule of law that, subject to being overruled by a higher court or a statute, a decision of a court is binding and cannot be ignored or set aside by anyone, and least of all by members of the government who disagree with it. In *M v Home Office* [1992] QB 270, at 314–15 Nolan LJ adopted Stephen Sedley QC's submission that 'the proper constitutional relationship of the executive with the courts is that the courts will respect all acts of the executive within its lawful province, and that the executive will respect all decisions of the court as to what its lawful province is'. Accordingly, a statutory provision which confers power on a minister to override a decision of a court will be subjected to strict and intensive review. The exercise of the power will be unlawful without 'the clearest possible justification' and 'properly explained and solid reasons': *R (Evans) v Attorney-General* [2015] UKSC 21 at [91] and [129].

*Evans's* case concerned section 53 of the Freedom of Information Act 2000, which empowered a minister to issue a certificate stating that he or she had on reasonable grounds formed the opinion that there was no failure to comply with a request for the information, the effect of which would be to override a decision of the Information Commissioner or of the Upper Tribunal. In that case, the Attorney-General issued a certificate under section 53 which would have had the effect of overriding a decision of the Upper Tribunal ordering disclosure of certain communications (the 'black spider' memos) between the Prince of Wales and government departments. The tribunal's decision had not been appealed and the tension between Parliamentary Sovereignty (see 6–7) and the requirements of the rule of law was evident. Five justices of the Supreme Court held that the certificate was invalid and unlawful because it did not engage with the closely reasoned analysis of the Upper Tribunal. Three of them went further, concluding at [52] and [58]–[59] that section 53 fell far short of being 'crystal clear' in authorising a member of the executive to override the decision of a court because he disagreed with it. Two justices dissented on the ground, as one stated at [154], that 'it is an integral part of the rule of law that courts give effect to Parliamentary intention'.

In Britain, all the institutions of our state originated in the monarchy. For this reason, as foreshadowed in chapter one and perhaps unsurprisingly, save for the independence of the judiciary and the power of the courts to supervise the legality of the acts of government and other public bodies by judicial review, our constitution has not clearly recognised separation of powers as a constitutional principle. Lord Simon of Glaisdale stated that what we have is:

> not separation of powers but something far more subtle and far more valuable – a balance of powers. It is no use separating your executive if it has powers over the individual which are considered inordinate. The executive's powers should be balanced by that of the legislature and the judicature. That is threatened by advocacy of a system purely based on separation of powers. It is a balance of powers that will vouchsafe liberty of the subject and individual rights: HL Debs, vol 597, col 719, 17 February 1999.

Lord Lloyd was more hostile, stating that the 'freedom of the citizen in the United Kingdom is guaranteed by the Rule of Law, not the separation of powers': evidence to HC Constitutional Affairs Committee 2004, §20.

Walter Bagehot, the nineteenth-century political analyst and journalist, famously stated that the 'nearly complete fusion of legislative and executive powers' is the efficient secret of the English Constitution. It was a secret because in the mid-nineteenth century the true position was masked by three factors. These were: the greater independence of Members of Parliament from control by their parties; the power of the House of Lords to veto legislation; and the existence of constitutional conventions, non-legal rules of political conduct generally observed, but principally subject only to political control. The greater independence, power of veto and the general observance of conventions operated as checks on the executive and fostered a system of accountability. In 1765 Blackstone was able to state that each branch of the state is 'armed with a negative power sufficient to repel any innovation which it shall think inexpedient or dangerous': *Commentaries*, vol 1 at 9.

Today, irrespective of whether or not the last half century has seen the transformation of Cabinet government into Prime Ministerial government, the position differs. Although our constitution is now far more democratic because of the extension of the franchise between 1832 and 1928 when universal adult suffrage was established, it is far less balanced. The House of Lords no longer has a veto over legislation. The combination of a 'first past the post' electoral system for UK Parliamentary elections, and the strength of the party system where MPs generally follow the line indicated by their party whip, means that the executive generally controls the legislative process.

There is an undoubted need for the executive to be able to exercise power effectively and efficiently. As Blackstone said in the context of the conduct of foreign affairs, power is generally 'wisely placed in a single hand by the British constitution, for the sake of unanimity, strength and despatch': *Commentaries*, vol 1 232-243. But, the exercise of power has to be within the law and, given Parliamentary sovereignty, with the executive self-restraint which constitutes one of the essential underpinnings of democracy and the rule of law: Daintith and Page, at 380. The greater central control represented by the move towards Prime Ministerial government together with reforms of public service such as increased outsourcing with the stated aim of increasing effectiveness and efficiency has, however, meant that the internal controls within the executive and its own self-restraint have been weakened.

Political scientists consider that 'the most serious of all contemporary constitutional challenges [is] how in a democratic society ... the executive power is to be restrained and kept within bounds' and that parliamentary sovereignty 'provides a cloak of legitimacy for executive and party dominance': see respectively, Professor Nevil Johnson, at 5 and former MP Tony Wright, at 6. Save for the periods (see 137) in which there was a minority or a coalition government, it is the case, as Peter Hennessy observed at 142, that 'ours is very much the executive's constitution'. Johnson considered (at 16) that the reason the executive needs to be restrained is that sound institutional practices once thought binding are in a state of decay because of 'the obsessive pursuit of party manifesto promises and the pursuit of sectional interests at the expense of the interests of the wider majority'. The fundamental imbalance between the executive and the legislature in our constitution is one of the reasons for increased recourse to the courts, and increased success in such recourse since the late 1960s. The imbalance was not addressed by any of the reforms since 1997. For instance, although the House of Lords Act 1999 disqualified the vast majority of hereditary peers from sitting and voting, no further steps have been taken to make it a more democratically accountable body. It remains a largely appointed body with an unwieldy number of members.

The result is that, leaving aside the question of any movement to a more direct form of democracy, the institutional arrangements which, as a result of Parliamentary sovereignty, generally produce the 'elective dictatorship' referred to at 6, sit uncomfortably with two of the guiding principles of the UK's constitutional arrangements. One is the rule of law. The other is access to justice and to an independent and impartial judiciary. The discomfort arises if sovereignty means Parliament may by statute oust the supervisory jurisdiction of the High Court over a government minister, a regulatory body or an inferior court, That has not been determined, although in *Privacy International* at [144], discussed further in chapter nine at 145, three members of the Supreme Court considered that there is 'a strong case for holding that, consistently with the rule of law', it could not.

For these reasons, it is premature to claim, as Vernon Bogdanor, 285 has, that the consequence of the constitutional reforms implemented since 1997 'may be summarised by saying that the idea of sovereignty of parliament has been replaced by that of the separation of powers, so putting Britain on the path to becoming a genuine constitutional state'. But the attempt to move beyond Dicey's purely descriptive use (at 89) of the term 'constitutional statute' since Laws LJ's judgment in *Thoburn v Sunderland CC* [2002] EWHC 195 (Admin) suggests one possible doctrinal way forward.

## II. CONSTITUTIONAL STATUTES

In the case of statutes recognised as 'constitutional', there is a presumption that Parliament intended to legislate in conformity with them and not to undermine them, and thus to exclude the usual doctrine of implied repeal by later inconsistent legislation. The Divisional Court in *Miller 1*, in a phrase resonant of the principle of legality discussed at 34 and 141, described this as excluding 'casual implied repeal': [2016]

EWHC 2768 (Admin) at [88]. The effect of this approach has been said to give 'the statutory parts of the constitution ... the same degree of protection as the common law parts receive under the principle of legality': Ahmed and Perry, 462.

There is force in the suggestion by Professor Paul Craig 2017, 70 that 'a statute worthy of the denomination constitutional should not be rendered devoid of effect through recourse to the prerogative' in the way the government argued in *Miller 1* could be done in relation to the European Communities Act 1972. The crucial questions, however, are which statutes are 'constitutional' and whether there is a principled basis for distinguishing them from 'ordinary' statutes? For Laws LJ:

> [A] constitutional statute is one which (a) conditions the legal relationship between citizen and State in some general, overarching manner, or (b) enlarges or diminishes the scope of what we would now regard as fundamental constitutional rights. (a) and (b) are of necessity closely related: it is difficult to think of an instance of (a) that is not also an instance of (b). The special status of constitutional statutes follows the special status of constitutional rights: *Thoburn v Sunderland CC* at [62].

He gave as examples the Magna Carta, the Bill of Rights 1689, the Act of Union, the Reform Acts which distributed and enlarged the franchise, the HRA, and the devolution legislation. To his list can be added the CRA 2005. But the limited utility of lists is graphically illustrated by the fact that Laws LJ did not refer to the Northern Ireland legislation, and the devolution legislation to which he did refer was not included in the more recent list in *R (Buckinghamshire CC) v Transport Secretary* [2014] UKSC 3 (the 'HS2' case).

The HS2 case referred to 'constitutional instruments', and the majority in the Supreme Court in *Miller 1* did not use the term 'constitutional statute'. They refer to the 'profound' changes made by the European Communities Act 1972 which made EU law a new independent source of domestic UK law, the fundamentality of its changes to the UK's constitutional arrangements, and the further changes that would result from leaving the EU: [2017] UKSC 5 at [62]–[68]. The approaches are broadly similar to that of Laws LJ but give little further guidance. That in *Miller 1* has been criticised as imprecise (Elliott, at 264–68) and, save for *Thoburn's* case, the decisions have not identified any principle for determining which statutes are constitutional or contain fundamental principles.

Laws LJ's linkage of 'constitutional' status to fundamental rights has been criticised for three reasons: see Feldman, at 345–50 and 148 and Ahmed and Perry, at 465–71. First, this would only accord such status to rights regarded as 'fundamental' 'by force of the common law', as opposed to statute. Second, it is under-inclusive because it does not comfortably include statutes concerned with institutions of the state and their inter-relationship rather than those concerned with the relationship of the citizen and the state. Third, in including legislation concerned with the relationship between the citizen and the state the linkage may be over-inclusive because much legislation is concerned with that relationship.

Professor Feldman prefers an approach concentrating 'on the con-tribution of Acts, subordinate legislation, and individual provisions or groups of provisions to establishing institutions of the state, defining their roles and authority, and regulating their relationship with each other'. He considers that 'the key function of a constitution is … to con-stitute the state and its institutions and confer functions, powers and duties on them'. But others have observed that this is also over-inclusive because 'it is unlikely that full constitutional force can or should be given to every provision in a particular statute, even if it can be said in a general way that the statute is of constitutional importance': Sales 2016, at 100. Professors Ahmed and Perry advocate a test based on two elements. The first (similar to Feldman's) is whether the statute or part of it creates or regulates a state institution. The second is that the statute or the relevant part of it substantially influences what other state institutions may do.

It should also be noted that the jumping off point for Laws LJ's recognition of a category of 'constitutional' statutes was the recogni-tion by the common law of rights 'which should properly be classified as constitutional or fundamental': *Thoburn* at [62]. But, this may in itself be controversial. For example, Professor Dickson, chapter two, rejects the notion that the UK Supreme Court has recognised the concept of constitutional rights within the common law, although others are more optimistic: see some of the contributors to Elliott and Hughes. While the notion of 'constitutional' common law rights may well be conten-tious, earlier chapters have shown that many common law rights are so important or integral to the constitutional structure of the UK that they can properly be afforded a degree of special protection. It, how-ever, remains unclear which common law rights can be described as 'constitutional' or 'fundamental' and the extent of the protection they have. Laws LJ described rights which can be equated with rights con-tained in the ECHR as 'constitutional': *R v Lord Chancellor, ex p Lightfoot* [2000] QB 597, 609. But while the right to vote or the right to preserve the confidentiality of legal correspondence are likely to be recognised as 'constitutional', see *Watkins v Secretary of State for the Home Office* [2006] UKHL 17 at [25], the right not to suffer misfeasance in public office is unlikely to be.

Lord Sales 2016, at 99, has suggested extra-judicially that 'the courts should only identify a fundamental right or interest for the purposes of the principle of legality if it is plausible to infer that Parliament as a collective body itself recognises such a right or interest'. He considers that, in the long run, the most defensible concept of domestic fundamental rights is one which aims to identify common background understandings of both courts and the legislature. Although more promising, absent any special legislative process for constitutional legislation or recourse to what was said in debates or pre-legislative reports, in relation to statutes the first two of the tools he mentions – inferring constitutional force from the circumstances in which a particular piece of legislation was passed and the prominence it is given in constitutional debate – are also relatively open-textured.

For these reasons, it remains difficult to define the boundaries of the category in a principled manner. In its present state and, without further doctrinal development, the category of 'constitutional statutes' remains under-analysed and too fragile a category to show that Britain is now firmly on the path to becoming a genuine constitutional state.

# III. THE BALANCE OF RESPONSIBILITIES

The balance of powers referred to by Lord Simon can also be regarded as a balance of responsibilities. This section considers where courts properly have a primary or significant role and where they should abstain or be circumspect because the matter is a political question for government or one which the primary decision-maker is better equipped to make.

Courts have primacy over questions of law and have deployed powerful and restrictive principles of statutory construction limiting general words in statutes by relying on common law principles. In relation to individuals, they have done so to accord special protection to certain interests, notably that of access to the court and procedural fairness discussed in chapters six and nine, the presumption of legality discussed in chapters four, five and nine, and the prevention of arbitrariness discussed in chapter five.

As well as the protection of individual rights, courts have also protected the statutory and constitutional position of public bodies and institutions: *Miller 2 & Cherry*, at [40]. In traditional judicial review of a central/local dispute, they may have to decide who Parliament has made the primary decision-maker and to give close scrutiny to a decision by the body with secondary responsibility which appears to 'interfere' with the role and responsibilities of the primary decision-maker. In *Secretary of State for Education v Tameside MBC* [1977] AC 1014 the Secretary of State was held only to have residuary powers and only entitled to give directions to the local primary decision-maker if it had acted contrary to the *Wednesbury* principles. He was not entitled to direct a newly elected local education authority not to implement plans to convert a number of grammar schools to comprehensive schools. But in *Nottinghamshire CC v Secretary of State for the Environment* [1986] AC 240, on which see 66, the council's challenge to a reduction in its rate support grant failed because the Secretary of State's decision had primacy. Absent abuse of power, matters concerning levels of public expenditure and the incidence and distribution of tax were 'matters of political judgment for [the Secretary of State] and for the House of Commons', and not for the judges.

*Miller 1* and *Miller 2 & Cherry* concerned the court's role in the resolution of issues between the legislature and the executive. In both cases, the government had sought to exclude Parliament. In *Miller 1*, it argued that notice of the UK's intention to leave the EU did not require legislation and, in *Miller 2 & Cherry* that its decision to prorogue Parliament for a five week period was a political question for government and not justiciable in the courts. In both cases the court protected the constitutional role of Parliament in ensuring the accountability of the executive to it and that its own sovereignty was not circumvented by the use of the prerogative power.

In *Miller 1*, the dissenters considered that the legal accountability that resulted from the majority's approach unduly underplayed the role of democratic and political accountability and thus the role of the UK's political constitution. Lord Carnwath considered that the principle of parliamentary accountability was no less fundamental to the UK's constitution than parliamentary sovereignty: [249] and [254]. Lord Reed stated that '[i]t is important for courts to understand that the legalisation of political issues is not always constitutionally appropriate, and may be fraught with risk, not least for the judiciary': [240] and [161]. Notwithstanding the force of the dissenters' points, which Professor

Endicott has argued 'are unanswerable', the majority did not underplay the importance of democratic and political accountability. Their treatment of the devolution arguments, referred to at 12–13 and 23, showed they were fully aware of the limits of legal accountability. As they stated at [78], 'withdrawal from the EU effects a fundamental change in the constitutional arrangements of the [UK]' which affected legal rights by removing an independent and overriding source of UK domestic law. They concluded at [82] that a major change to the UK's constitutional arrangements could not be achieved by ministers alone and had to be effected 'in the only way that the UK constitution recognises, namely by Parliamentary legislation'.

In *Miller 2 & Cherry* at [34], [42] and [46] the Court considered that a non-justiciable and therefore unlimited power of prorogation would undermine, and be incompatible with, the legal principle of the sovereignty of Parliament as the foundational principle of the UK's constitution. Lengthy prorogation would also undermine the principle of Parliamentary accountability by which 'the policies of the executive are subjected to consideration by the representatives of the electorate, the executive is required to report, explain and defend its actions, and citizens are protected from the arbitrary exercise of executive power'. Setting a limit on the power to prorogue did not offend the separation of powers but gave effect to it by ensuring that government does not use the power of prorogation unlawfully. The court concluded:

> [A] decision to prorogue Parliament (or to advise the monarch to prorogue Parliament) will be unlawful if the prorogation has the effect of frustrating or preventing, without reasonable justification, the ability of Parliament to carry out its constitutional functions as a legislature and as the body responsible for the supervision of the executive.: [50]

Resolving tensions or disagreement between the executive and the legislature politically may be a difficult and lengthy process without a constitutional 'adjudicator' or a 'mediator'. The fact that over most of our recent history the executive has dominated and controlled the legislature has meant situations of tension and disagreement between the executive and the legislature rarely arise and thus they may have been overlooked when identifying the paradigm. It is not without significance that the seventeenth century, a time of tension and disagreement between the Crown and Parliament, was a century in which the courts were active: see for example the *Case of Proclamations* (1611) 12 Co Rep 74. It is true that neither of the *Miller* cases was prompted by what can be described as 'active disagreement' between the legislature and the executive. However, given the sharp difference of views about leaving the EU and how to give effect to the referendum result, the context of the litigation can fairly be described as one of tension and disagreement. Moreover, it would be wrong to characterise the approach of the Supreme Court as judicial usurpation of political power. The issue in both cases was whether it was open to the executive to prevent Parliament from having a meaningful role in the process.

The balance of responsibilities also means that some issues are regarded as not susceptible to resolution by a court or are ones where courts should show restraint or circumspection. The reasons for the former include the absence of judicial or manageable standards on which to judge an issue, or that the matter is a political question for government. The reasons for the latter include institutional competence or because the primary decision-maker is more fully equipped to make the decision than the court.

Issues not susceptible to resolution by a court include state immunity and foreign acts of state: see *Belhaj v Straw* [2017] UKSC 3, although, as seen at 41, its scope is difficult to define. They also include acts of state of the UK government on foreign policy including the deployment of the armed forces, and questions of religious belief which do not engage private rights. The former are beyond the courts' competence under the UK's conception of the separation of powers because the courts would be trespassing on the province of the executive as responsible for foreign affairs: *Rahmatullah v Ministry of Defence* [2016] UKSC 1. There is force in Blackstone's view (referred to at 119) that, in this context, power is generally 'wisely placed in a single hand by the British constitution, for the sake of unanimity, strength and despatch'. The truth of disputed tenets of religious belief is incapable of objective assessment by courts but, where contractual or property rights depend on religious issues, the court must determine such of them as are capable of objective ascertainment: *Shergill v Kharia* [2014] UKSC 33.

Two examples show the circumspection shown in relation to sensitive and deeply controversial social and ethical issues. In *Bellinger v Bellinger* [2003] UKHL 21 the court refused to use section 3 of the HRA to interpret the Matrimonial Causes Act 1973 so as to recognise the marriage of a transsexual person in their assumed gender as this would involve a major change to the law in a field of sensitive social policy. The court considered (at [37]) that the issues which required extensive enquiry and consultation were 'altogether ill-suited for determination by courts and court procedures'. They 'are pre-eminently a matter for Parliament', particularly where the government, in unequivocal terms, had already announced its intention to introduce comprehensive primary legislation. The court did, however, make a declaration of incompatibility and Parliament passed the Gender Recognition Act 2004.

Sometimes the nature of the issue will preclude even a finding of incompatibility. As stated in chapter one, in *R (Nicklinson) v Ministry of Justice* [2014] UKSC 38 the virtually unanimous view of the nine justices of the Supreme Court was that in principle Parliament was a better forum for determining the question of relaxing the blanket ban on assisted suicide in section 2 of the Suicide Act 1961. Two, however, considered that it was institutionally appropriate for the court to determine this and would have declared the blanket ban to be incompatible with the right to respect for private life guaranteed by ECHR article 8.

In *Nicklinson* four of the seven justices in the majority decided that the matter was one for Parliament and not the courts. The other three, however, contemplated that circumstances might arise in the future in which the court could hold that the blanket ban was incompatible with ECHR article 8. The complexity and difficulty of the issue was reflected by the variety of reasons given by the majority. They included that Parliament had repeatedly considered the blanket ban, that at the time of the hearing a bill on the question was before Parliament, and that it was not simple to identify a remedy for incompatibility while providing safeguards against abuse. The situation may be one in which, as Allan 2013, 184, observed, it is simply too hard for a court to define the exceptions to a statutory rule to accommodate marginal cases without jeopardising the rationale for the rule. Lord Mance stated at [190] that Parliament was the preferable forum in which any decision should be made, after full investigation and consideration, 'in a manner which will command popular acceptance'. He and two other justices considered Parliament should be given a further opportunity to reconsider and decide. The matter remains controversial. Subsequent attempts in three Bills to change the law failed. In *R (Conway) v Secretary of State for Justice* [2018] EWCA Civ 1431 the Court of Appeal held that Parliament is a far better body for determining this difficult policy issue, and the Supreme Court refused to consider a further appeal: [2018] UKSC B1.

Even on issues of social and ethical policy, courts will not simply abdicate. This is illustrated by a 2018 case before the Supreme Court on the prohibition of abortion in Northern Ireland legislation. A challenge to the prohibition failed because the claimant, which was a public interest group and not a victim of the law, did not have standing to institute abstract proceedings so that the court did not have jurisdiction. Nevertheless, a majority of the court stated that, had there been jurisdiction, they would have held that, insofar as abortion was prohibited in cases of rape, incest and fatal foetal abnormality, it was incompatible with ECHR article 8: *Re an application by the Northern Ireland Human Rights Commission for Judicial Review* [2018] UKSC 27. They would have made a declaration of incompatibility which would have placed the matter squarely with the legislature.

The majority distinguished *Nicklinson* and assisted suicide for four main reasons. First, in assisted suicide the issue was to balance the interests of the adult who wished to commit suicide with the protection of others who, whether through age or disability, might feel pressured by others to commit suicide. The abortion issue did not require such a balance to be struck. The balance was between the rights of pregnant women to decide what should be done with their own bodies and the community's interest in the regulation of pregnancy in circumstances where existing legislation recognised important limits on the interests and protection of the unborn foetus. Secondly, unlike *Nicklinson*, the incompatibility was not difficult to identify or to cure by amending the legislation to permit termination in the three situations. Thirdly, the UK's approach to assisted dying largely reflected the approach over the whole of Europe, whereas the abortion laws in Northern Ireland were almost alone in their strictness. Fourthly, the democratic institutions of Northern Ireland had not firmly expressed a view on the question.

In a powerful dissent, Lord Reed stated:

> it is difficult to envisage a more controversial issue than the proper limits of the law governing abortion. Diametrically opposed views, and every shade of opinion in between, are held with equal sincerity and conviction. Each side of the debate appeals to moral or religious values which are held with passionate intensity. In a democracy on the British model, the natural place for that debate to be resolved is in the legislature: at [336].

He considered that the acceptance in the ECHR that rights under article 8 are subject to such limitations as are 'necessary in a democratic society' opens the door to democratic policy choices: see [340]. The HRA and the devolution statutes did not alter 'the inherent limitations of court proceedings as a means of determining issues of social and ethical policy' nor 'the inappropriateness, and the dangers for the courts themselves, of highly contentious issues being determined by judges, who have neither any special insight into such questions nor any political accountability for their decisions'. Although there was no decision by a court on the point, the law was changed by legislation in 2019; and because of the breakdown of the devolution arrangements in Northern Ireland between 2017 and 2020 it was done in regulations made by the UK government.

As seen in chapter five, judges have shown circumspection in the exercise of the court's judicial review jurisdiction over certain discretionary powers although, again they do not abdicate and leave the field entirely to the primary decision-maker. Courts have stated that they will be constrained where the decision is about how to allocate scarce resources, or where the form of an adversarial hearing means they cannot confidently draw general conclusions.

So, judgments as to how best to allocate limited medical resources to the maximum advantage of the greatest number of patients have been said not to be ones which a court can make: *R v Cambridge DHA, ex p B* [1995] 1 WLR 898, 906. Nor are questions of which magistrates' courts in an area to close, see 75, or as to financial and economic policy or national security, see 66–68. This is because these decisions are polycentric in the sense that a decision on one matter, in the *Cambridge* case not to provide expensive treatment to a child with cancer, will affect other decisions, in that case, the availability of treatment for other patients. *Bellinger v Bellinger*, considered above, is an example of constraint resulting from the limitations of adversarial hearings as well as the sensitivity of the policy issues.

The courts also show restraint where the challenge is to predictive decisions such as risk assessments on questions involving national security, terrorism, and public disorder: see 67–68. The position is similar for assessments concerning scientific and technical questions. In *R (Mott) v Environment Agency* [2016] EWCA Civ 564 it was stated that the adequacy of a model used to estimate percentages of fish originating from a given river 'is more a matter of scientific judgment than legal analysis'. A reviewing court should therefore be very slow to conclude that the expert decision-maker assigned the task by statute has reached a perverse scientific conclusion.

Even though questions of law are generally for courts to determine, *R v Monopolies and Mergers Commission, ex p South Yorkshire Transport*

[1993] 1 WLR 23 shows that circumspection may be shown on a question of law if the underlying concept and the statutory language used to identify it are very imprecise. The Commission had jurisdiction to investigate mergers which affected 'a substantial part of the UK' and, taking account of factors such as the social, political and economic significance of the area and its geography, concluded that it had jurisdiction over the merger of certain bus companies in South Yorkshire. The companies challenged the decision because the area affected was only 1.65 per cent of the UK's surface area and 3.4 per cent of its population.

The court (at 29–30) held that the word 'substantial' was a jurisdictional question with one legally correct meaning. But because the word was so imprecise that different decision-makers acting rationally might reach different conclusions when applying it to the facts of a given case the court stated that it would be wrong to thrust on it 'a spurious degree of precision'. It concluded (at 32) that the court could 'substitute its own opinion for that of the person to whom the decision has been entrusted only if the decision is so aberrant that it cannot be classed as rational'. This is to use the concept of error of law as a façade behind which to consider factors such as relative expertise of the court and the public authority entrusted with primary responsibility for the decision, in that case the Commission. Compare Endicott 1998, at 317–319, who considers that, on a sound analytic approach, a question of the application of statutory language is truly a question of law only when the law requires one answer to it.

The importance of the court exercising its power circumspectly and taking account of factors other than a purely linguistic or textual analysis of the statute is also shown in the Supreme Court's decision in *R (Cart) v Upper Tribunal* [2011] UKSC 28. The court recognised (at [57], [61], [64] and [68]) that in the case of the Upper Tribunal, by statute a superior court of record, considerations of proportionality justified a more restrained approach to judicial review. It considered (see [41]–[42] and [89]) that there must be a limit to the resources which the legal system can devote to getting the result right in any individual case. As appeals lie from the Upper Tribunal to the Court of Appeal on important points of principle or practice or where there is some other compelling reason, the arrangements for the administration of justice adequately protected the rule of law by ensuring that important errors could be corrected. Accordingly, a broad approach to the availability of judicial review would result in an unnecessary and unwarranted duplication of judicial process.

There are differing views as to the degree to which a court should display circumspection, exactly where to draw the line and, whether, in a particular case, a court has overstepped it. The need for there to be some independent institution to determine what is required by law makes total abstention problematic from the point of view of both the rule of law and the separation of powers. But the earlier discussion shows that courts are generally appropriately sensitive to the need for judicial abstention or circumspection in certain circumstances. It will be needed where there are no judicial or manageable standards on which to decide an issue, where the matter is a political question for the democratically accountable branches of the state, or where the primary decision-maker's institutional and factual expertise on a question means that it is better equipped to make the decision.

# 9

# Enabling Majorities and Protecting Minorities in Our Democracy

The assumption underlying a modern democratic state is that generally laws are passed, and decisions taken, on the basis of the views of the majority. The philosopher John Rawls assumed that 'some form of majority rule is justified as the best way of insuring just and effective legislation' and that 'a fundamental part of the majority principle is that [it] should satisfy the conditions of background justice': Rawls, 356. But, as has also been said, '[t]he great problem of democratic political and legal thought has been the reconciliation of popular will with individual rights and, in particular, of the rights of the majority with those of the minority': Friedmann, 419–20.

There are two ways in which the UK's constitutional arrangements enable majorities. The first is the requirement to hold regular elections to the legislature in which the franchise, that is those entitled to vote, is almost universal. The second is the principle of Parliamentary sovereignty referred to in earlier chapters, which applies to the UK Parliament at Westminster but not to the devolved Parliaments. Our system of representative government also occasionally resorts to referendums on major issues, such as the creation of the devolved Parliaments or where, as in the case of membership of the EU, there are divisions within parties.

By majorities, I mean those whose voices and values are given effect to in the regular political process and are thus reflected in legislative and regulatory regimes. By minorities, I mean those individuals and groups whose voices and values are not given effect to and are not reflected in legislative and regulatory regimes. In considering the claims of majorities and minorities, it is relevant to consider whether our system is a 'winner takes all' system, or whether there are or should be legal or political limits on the extent to which 'to the victor belong the spoils'.

In his second Reith Lecture, 'In Praise of Politics', when considering the respective spheres of law and politics, Lord Sumption stated that the great dilemma of modern democracies is how to control 'the potentially oppressive power of democratic majorities without undermining democracy itself'. In this he echoes the views of Friedmann above and of Nevil Johnson and the other political scientists referred to, at 119. But, perhaps because in 2019 there was, atypically, a deeply divided minority government which needed to find consensus, he appears to have had more confidence in the potential of politics as a control than them or Lord Radcliffe another judge who gave the Reith Lectures. In his 1951 lectures, Lord Radcliffe stated that 'carried to its logical conclusion, Parliament is turned into the instrument of power instead of being its holder'. Whichever analysis is correct, the recognition that there is potential for oppression or overreaching makes it important to identify what rights, interests and values should be allowed to trump the policy objectives of those who won the last election and are in power at the relevant time.

# I. THE RIGHT TO VOTE AT REGULAR ELECTIONS

The right to vote has long been regarded as important and effectively a property right. Electors denied a vote have been awarded damages against returning officers despite claims of privilege by Parliament: *Turner v Sterling* 1671 2 Vent 25 and *Ashby v White* (1703) 1 Smiths LC 253, 283. In *Hipperson v Newbury District Electoral Registration Officer* [1985] QB 1060, 1067 Sir John Donaldson MR stated that 'voting rights lie at the root of Parliamentary democracy. Indeed, many would regard them as a basic human right'. Today they are recognised as a basic or constitutional right, and the principle of legality should apply to construing any statute affecting the right to vote: *Watkins v Home Office* [2006] UKHL 17 at [61].

In the century after the Reform Act 1832, rights to vote were extended by a series of Acts of Parliament. There is now universal adult suffrage, except for those convicted of corrupt or illegal practices at elections, those who lack legal capacity, those who are disenfranchised because they are serving a prison sentence and, in the case of the UK Parliament, members of the House of Lords.

ECHR Article 3 of Protocol No 1 sets out the right to free elections in the choice of the legislature. It includes the right to vote, subject to lawful and proportionate limitations, but it does not apply to referendums. The common law has not, however, recognised a right of universal and equal suffrage from which any derogation must be provided for by law and must be proportionate: *Moohan v Lord Advocate* [2014] UKSC 67 at [33]–[34]. Lord Hodge, with whom four other members of the Supreme Court agreed, stated that it is Parliament which determines and controls the franchise and it is not appropriate for the courts to develop the common law in order to supplement or override the statutory rules which determine our democratic franchise. Accordingly, they rejected a challenge to a ban in an Act of the Scottish Parliament on serving prisoners voting in the 2014 referendum on Scottish Independence.

The disenfranchisement of all serving prisoners notwithstanding Article 3 of Protocol No 1 led to a major difference between the UK and the Council of Europe and the Strasbourg Court. *Hirst v UK (No 2)* (2006) 42 EHRR 41 decided, and *Scoppola v Italy (No 3)* (2013) 56 EHRR 19 confirmed, that the bar in section 3(1) of the Representation of the People Act 1983 violated that right. The strength of feeling in the UK meant UK governments did not then take forward proposals to change the law even though explicitly required to in 2010. Although in *R (Chester) v Justice Secretary* [2013] UKSC 63 the Supreme Court held that that it was bound to follow the law as stated in the Strasbourg decisions, it did not make a declaration of invalidity because one had already been made in 2007 by Scotland's highest civil appeal court, the Inner House of the Court of Session sitting as the Registration Appeal Court: *Smith v Scott* [2007] CSIH 9. In *Chester's* case Lord Mance stated that it was 'now for Parliament as the democratically elected legislature to complete its consideration of the position'.

Ultimately the dispute was resolved in different ways in different parts of the UK. In Scotland, the Scottish Elections (Franchise and Representation) Act 2020, section 3, amending section 3(1A) of the 1983 UK Act has made convicted prisoners serving a sentence of 12 months or less eligible to vote. The UK Government proposed limited changes in administrative guidance in England and Wales, in particular to allow prisoners on temporary licence to vote. It considered these complied with the decision in *Hirst* 'in a way that respects the clear direction of successive Parliaments and the strong views of the British public' (630 HC Deb, cols 1007-8, 2 November 2017) and, in the light of the wide margin of appreciation allowed to Member States, the Council of Europe agreed.

*Moohan v Lord Advocate* is also of interest because, while stating that the common law cannot extend the franchise beyond that provided by parliamentary legislation, the majority did not exclude the possibility of a further situation arising in which it might ultimately be for the courts rather than the legislature to determine the common law limits to legislative power. In the context of the legislation of the non-sovereign unicameral Scottish Parliament, the majority did not 'exclude the possibility that, in the very unlikely event that a parliamentary majority abusively sought to entrench its power by a curtailment of the franchise or similar device, the common law, informed by principles of democracy and the rule of law and international norms, would be able to declare such legislation unlawful'. It has been suggested that restricting the 'exceptional circumstances' review referred to in *Jackson's* case, on which see 8–9, 'to unicameral legislatures which have suffered a severe breakdown in the deliberative process reflects the strong claims to legitimacy possessed by the legislative process when contrasted with the common law supervisory jurisdiction': Hooper, 22.

Since 1911 the maximum period between elections to the UK Parliament has been five years, although legislation extended this by a year at a time during the two World Wars. Legislation extending the maximum duration of Parliament requires the consent of both Houses. Until 2011 Prime Ministers had the politically important power to advise the Monarch to dissolve the UK Parliament and call an early election, but that flexibility was removed by the Fixed Term Parliaments Act 2011. That Act requires a five-year period between general elections and permits earlier elections only if two-thirds of the House of Commons agree, or there has been a vote of no confidence in the government and no alternative government is confirmed within 14 days. On 1 December 2020, a draft Bill providing for its repeal was presented to Parliament: see CM 322.

The examination of systems for ascertaining majorities and their democratic legitimacy falls outside the scope of this book. Suffice it to say that the UK has fragmented electoral systems. The devolved institutions have systems of proportional representation whereas the UK Parliament remains a 'first past the post' constituency-based system.

At the UK level, since 1919 there have been 13 Conservative governments, 11 Labour governments, two national governments and two
coalition governments. Between 1900 and 1945 the dominant form of
government was either coalition because of war or economic emergency or a minority government where the largest party relied on looser
arrangements with smaller parties on particular issues. Since 1945 the
system has resulted in clear single-party majorities for one of the two
dominant parties on all but four occasions. The constituency system
means that there can be a single-party majority without the winning
party receiving an overall majority of votes cast.

The system has produced a majority for a single party with just over
two-fifths of the votes. There were landslide majorities of over 100 for the
Conservatives in 1983 and 1987 with just over 42 per cent of the votes,
and for Labour in 1997 and 2001 with 43 per cent of the votes. The system also produced clear majorities for Labour in 2005 with 36 per cent
of the vote and for the Conservatives in 1992 with 41 per cent of the vote.
Only in 1931 and 1935 did the winning party get more than 50 per cent
of the votes. The highest percentage since 1945 is 49.7 per cent in 1955.
The divisions shown by these figures, and the ebbs and flows in the for-
tunes of parties over the last 100 years, provide support for the view that
it is legitimate for there to be a legal or political brake on the power of
the party that is in power for the time being. Apart from providing some
protection to certain rights of those who are out of power, such a brake
may be conducive to stability over time.

# II. PARLIAMENTARY SOVEREIGNTY

In the case of the UK, the major obstacle to such a brake is the force of the
principle of Parliamentary sovereignty, the foundational principle of the
UK's constitution, considered in chapters one and eight, and referred to
in others. As classically formulated, it is seen as authorising and enabling
the enactment of all laws and policies supported by those who voted
for the democratically elected government, including the hypothetical
statute mentioned by Dicey requiring all blue-eyed babies to be killed.
It should not, however, be forgotten that the principle was forged in
the aftermath of a Civil War and the military defeat of the Crown by
Parliament at a time when the franchise was limited. It was then seen as

a means for controlling the Monarch and ensuring that he ruled through the consent of Parliament. This is apparent from the focus of the Bill of Rights 1689. Articles I, II, IV, VIII and IX respectively declared it to be illegal for the Crown to suspend or dispense with laws or to levy taxation without the consent of Parliament; that elections ought to be free; and that 'freedom of speech and debate or proceedings in Parliament ought not to be impeached in any court or place out of Parliament'.

Sir Ivor Jennings 1959, 38 described the supremacy of Parliament as the most important principle of the constitution. As to its source, he stated that it:

> is no doubt a rule of the common law. It was not established by judicial decisions, however; it was settled by armed conflict and the Bill of Rights and the Act of Settlement. The judges did no more than acquiesce in a simple fact of political authority, though they have never been called upon precisely to say so.

# III. PARLIAMENT'S HISTORICAL ACQUIESCENCE IN COMMON LAW PRINCIPLES

Just as the judges acquiesced in a simple fact of political authority, so Parliament acquiesced in the principles of the common law that the courts had identified and applied in decisions before the constitutional changes that resulted from Parliament's victory in the English Civil War and in the next 100 years. Sir Frederick Pollock, at 165, observed that '[t]he omnipotence of Parliament was not the orthodox theory of English law, if orthodox at all, even in Holt's time'.

What then was it to which Parliament acquiesced? Sir Stephen Sedley 2015 has demonstrated the longstanding nature of four constitutional fundamentals. By the time of the seventeenth-century constitutional settlement it had been established that the courts had power to strike down decisions of public bodies which had acted without jurisdiction. The precursors to the principles of *Wednesbury* unreasonableness and *Padfield* impropriety of purpose used to control discretionary power discussed in chapter five are two sixteenth-century cases. By the mid-eighteenth century, it was established that courts had power to strike down decisions made without jurisdiction notwithstanding a statutory 'ouster' clause which appeared to prohibit this.

The *Case of the Marshalsea* (1613) 10 Co Rep 686 illustrates the first of these. The Court of the Marshalsea had jurisdiction only where one of the parties to a dispute was a member of the Royal Household, but neither of the parties in the case was a member of the Household. The court held that officers of the court who executed an order for the detention of the guarantor of a civil debtor were liable for assault and false imprisonment because they acted without jurisdiction.

The sixteenth-century precursors to *Wednesbury* unreasonableness and *Padfield* impropriety of purpose are *Rooke's Case* (1598) 5 Co Rep 99b and the *Case of Monopolies, Darcy v Allein* (1599) 11 Co Rep 84. In *Rooke's Case* commissioners of sewers imposed the entire cost of repairing a riverbank on the riparian owner, with the result that his neighbours benefited without contributing to its cost. The decision was set aside as not within 'the rule of reason and law' because the commissioners' discretion was 'not to do according to their wills and private affections'. In the *Case of Monopolies*, a monopoly to make and import playing cards granted to Darcy by Queen Elizabeth I was held to be contrary to common law. One of the grounds on which the court so held was that, when granting it, the Queen intended it to be for the public good because restricting the availability of cards would discourage a bad habit and reduce the number of people being distracted from their employment. Because Darcy permitted an excessive number of cards to circulate, he was held to be using the monopoly for his private gain and to the prejudice of the purpose of the Queen and the public good.

As to the approach to ouster clauses, *R v Derbyshire JJ* (1759) 2 Kenyon 299 concerned a statute of William & Mary prohibiting 'quashing any order made by virtue of this Act'. Despite this the court quashed an order made at the General Quarter Sessions requiring those who had been highway surveyors several years earlier to make over the balance of funds they held to the person who was now the highway surveyor because the Quarter Sessions did not have jurisdiction to make it. The 1969 decision of the House of Lords in *Anisminic v Foreign Compensation Commission* [1969] 2 AC 147, discussed at 44 and 144 which treated an ouster clause in the same way is seen by some as an example of judicial overreach and inconsistent with the principle of the sovereignty of Parliament. They, however, give insufficient weight to this history and to the nineteenth-century cases to the same effect which were analysed by Browne J at first instance in *Anisminic*: see [1969] 2 AC at 223 and Wade (1969) 27 CLJ 230.

The protection given to personal liberty and bodily integrity by the torts of false imprisonment and assault in decisions such as *Rooke's* case reflect rights of personal security and of personal liberty, two of the rights in English law that Blackstone identified as 'founded on nature and reason': *Commentaries* I, 127, 129. Another is the right to private property. A person's property is protected by the law of trespass: interfering with it without the owner's authority is a civil wrong, a tort. So, in *Entick* v *Carrington* (1765) 19 St Tr 1029, 1066 Lord Camden CJ stated that property is 'preserved sacred and incommunicable' save where it is abridged by Parliament. 'No man can set his foot upon my ground without my license, but he is liable to an action ... [and] ... he is bound to show by way of justification, that some positive law has empowered or excused him'.

In *Entick* v *Carrington* the Secretary of State argued that he had power to issue a warrant to enter and search Entick's house and to seize seditious papers and pamphlets because 'such warrants have been issued frequently' and 'this power is essential to government' and the only means available for 'quieting clamours and sedition'. The court rejected this.

Lord Camden asked 'what would the parliament say, if the judges should take upon themselves to mould an unlawful power into a convenient authority, by new restrictions? That would be, not judgment, but legislation'. The case also has some resonance in relation to press freedom. Its principle is reflected in Dicey's view of the rule of law as absence of arbitrary power. That Dicey, 247–48, considered provided a reason why 'liberty of the press has been long reputed as a special feature of English institutions' and why government has no authority to seize books and pamphlets because it considers that they contain seditious or libellous matter: Rowbottom in Tomkins and Scott, at 85 and 105ff.

The context in which these general common law principles were forged by the courts included instruments such as clauses 39 and 40 of Magna Carta and the Bill of Rights 1688. Clauses 39 and 40 respectively provided that no free man was to be 'seized, imprisoned, dispossessed [of property], outlawed, [or] exiled' save by authority of the law, and enunciated the right of access to the courts, discussed in chapter six. Article 10 of the Bill of Rights prohibits 'cruel and unusual punishment'.

The foundations for what is today generally known as the principle of legality, discussed at 34, were also laid before the seventeenth-century constitutional settlement. They can be traced back to a wider principle applied in *Stradling* v *Morgan* (1560) 1 Plow 199 that general statements in statutes are construed as having a narrower application than their literal meaning might suggest if that would produce an unjust result and in particular would override basic individual rights. The importance of the principle of legality is that the powers and duties of public authorities are primarily to be found in statutes. Although sometimes stated as a substantive principle, the principle of legality is, as Lord Hoffmann stated in *RB (Algeria) v Home Secretary* [2009] UKHL 10, in the end a rule of construction which cannot displace the plain and obvious meaning of the legislation, whether by express words or as a result of necessary implication.

Another principle is the presumption that Parliament does not legislate in a legal vacuum. Statutes are drafted on the basis that the ordinary rules and principles of the common law apply to express statutory provisions unless excluded expressly or by necessary implication. In *Cooper v Wandsworth Board of Works* (1863) 14 CB(NS) 180, 194, a local authority started to demolish a house without giving the owner notice of its intention, relying on a statutory power to do so. The statute did not expressly require the owner to be given an opportunity to explain himself but Byles J stated 'that, although there are no positive words in a statute requiring that the party shall be heard, yet the justice of the common law will supply the omission of the legislature'.

It remains the case that where a statute is silent, or uses general words, the courts will not imply a rule inconsistent with the rules and principles on which the common law is based. In that way, those rules and principles will affect the meaning of the statute. Accordingly, even if Parliament is ultimately sovereign, because statutes are drafted in this way it is constitutionally legitimate for courts to ensure that important common law rights, interests and values are only interfered with by clear language in the way described by Lord Hoffmann in *R v Home Secretary, ex p Simms* [2000] 2 AC 115 at 131, with Parliament squarely confronting what it is doing and accepting the political cost. He also stated that the presumption that 'even the most general words were intended to be subject to the basic rights of the individual' was the way that UK courts, 'although acknowledging the sovereignty of Parliament, apply principles of constitutionality little different from those which exist in countries where the power of the legislature is expressly limited by a constitutional document'. Earlier, in *R v Home Secretary, ex p Pierson* [1998] AC 539 at 598, Lord Steyn had said 'unless there is the clearest provision to the contrary, Parliament must be presumed not to legislate contrary to the rule of law'.

# IV.  LIMITATIONS ON THE PROTECTION OF MINORITIES

Save in one respect, however, the protection of the minority on any issue as a result of the application of common law rights is limited. Firstly, whether common-law basic rights and liberties are seen as residual or not, Parliamentary sovereignty generally means that a sufficiently explicit statute will limit or remove them. This is generally also so in the case of what are now called 'constitutional statutes'. For that reason, the rule of law as a principle of legality has been able to function as a guardian, but not a guarantor, of civil liberties and fundamental rights. This was particularly evident in the period between 1914 and 1945 which can now be seen as the twilight period of English public law.

Writing about legislation which restricted personal and political liberties passed between those years, Ewing and Gearty argue there is not a single case of significance in the Law Reports of the judicial power of interpretation being used to limit its scope. That is no longer the case but, in that period, interpretation sometimes did the exact opposite by giving statutory words a strained meaning which broadened the scope of the power conferred and unduly restricted basic rights.

The infamous decision in *Liversidge v Anderson* [1942] AC 206, now acknowledged to be wrong, concerned Defence Regulation 18B. The regulation authorised the detention of a person whom the Home Secretary 'has reasonable cause to believe' is of hostile origin or associations rather than, as had been originally proposed, if he was 'satisfied that it is necessary' to detain. On orthodox principles of statutory construction, the words 'reasonable cause' would have required the Home Secretary's belief to be based on objective grounds. However, the House of Lords held that they authorised detention where the Home Secretary's belief was subjective, irrespective of the reasonableness of that belief, and that no evidence was needed from him to justify the decision to detain. In a famous dissent, now recognised as correct, Lord Atkin stated that the only authority which might justify the subjective construction of the majority was the exchange in *Through the Looking Glass* where Humpty Dumpty told Alice that when he used a word 'it means just what I choose it to mean, neither more nor less'.

The second reason that the protection of minorities is limited is that the common law may be unable to protect their rights or may be too ready to impose unnecessary or pointless limitations on them. In *Entick v Carrington* the protection came as a result of the wrongful interference with *Entick's* property rights, but the exercise of public power might not be a violation of a recognised personal or property right, or a legally protected interest. *Duncan v Jones* [1936] 1 KB 218, 222 concerned a meeting outside a training centre for the unemployed, at which a speaker was arrested on the ground that the police reasonably apprehended a breach of the peace if the meeting were held. Lord Hewart LCJ stated that 'English law does not recognise any special right of public meeting for political or other purposes' and held that the police acted lawfully. Again, *Malone's* case, discussed at 63, held that there was no right of privacy and no other individual right existed which could protect a citizen from the police tapping his telephone in the exercise of a broad discretionary power. In *Kaye v Robertson* [1991] FSR 62, Sunday Sport journalists burst into a hospital room without authority and interviewed and photographed a well-known actor recovering from brain surgery. The actor was in no fit condition to give informed consent to be interviewed or photographed but the court held that the newspaper could not be restrained from publishing the interview and photographs.

As to unnecessary or pointless limitations to a basic freedom, the clearest example concerns freedom of expression and a book, *Spycatcher*, by a retired intelligence officer which alleged wrongdoing by the Security Service. The UK government obtained injunctions restraining its publication and any articles about it, but the injunctions were discharged after the book was published in the United States. By the time the English proceedings reached the House of Lords it was selling like 'hot cakes' in a number of countries and copies were circulating in the UK. Despite this, in *Attorney-General v Guardian Newspapers Ltd (No 1)* [1987] 1 WLR 1248 a majority of the House of Lords reinstated the injunction. They justified this as necessary to protect the secrecy of the Security Service within the UK, but there is considerable force in the views of the two dissenting judges. Lord Bridge stated that the maintenance of the ban, as more and more copies of the book circulated in the UK, 'will seem more and more ridiculous'. Lord Oliver stated that in the circumstances of the case the injunctions could not be justified 'constitutionally and in the public interest in a free society'.

# V. ATTEMPTS TO EXCLUDE ACCESS TO THE ORDINARY COURTS

The only common law right which may survive an apparently clear statutory attempt to exclude it is the right of access to the ordinary courts discussed in chapter six. *Anisminic v Foreign Compensation Commission* [1969] 2 AC 147 was a challenge to the Commission's decision that *Anisminic* was not eligible to participate in a compensation fund for British entities who suffered loss from the acts of a foreign government. The difficulty was that section 4 of the Foreign Compensation Act 1950 provided that any determination by the Commission 'shall not be called into question in any court of law', a provision expressly exempted from section 11 of the Tribunals and Inquiries Act 1958 which provided that such clauses were ineffective to exclude the supervisory jurisdiction of the High Court by way of judicial review, as does section 12 of the identically named Act of 1992.

The House of Lords held that section 4 did not preclude judicial review where, in Lord Reid's words, the Commission misconstrued the provisions giving it power to act 'so that it failed to deal with the question remitted to it and decided some question which was not remitted to it'. Such a decision was a 'purported determination' but not a valid one. Lord Wilberforce asked 'what would be the purpose of defining by statute the limit of a tribunal's powers, if, by means of a clause inserted in the defining statute, those limits could safely be passed'. In later cases, Lord Diplock said that 'for practical purposes' all errors of law will deprive a public body of its jurisdiction: *Re Racal Communications Ltd.* [1981] 1 AC 374, 382 and *O'Reilly v Mackman* [1983] 2 AC 237, 278. The result is that the court reviewing the decision will generally determine the meaning of the statutory provision and substitute its judgment for that of the primary decision-maker.

It is interesting to note that the Parliamentary reaction to *Anisminic* was not to seek to reverse the decision by finding a formula that would reinstate the absolute ouster of the court's jurisdiction. Section 3 of the Foreign Compensation Act 1969 provided a right of appeal to the Court of Appeal on any question relating to the Commission's jurisdiction, and thus preserved access to the court. In a sense, what happened can be seen as a dialogue between court and legislature similar to the one contemplated today when a court makes a declaration under section 4 of the HRA that a statutory provision is incompatible with ECHR rights, leaving it to Parliament to decide what to do. There were similar dialogues after proposals in the Asylum and Immigration (Treatment of Claimants) Bill 2004 to remove any right of appeal or review from the Immigration Appeal Tribunal and in the Internal Market Bill 2020 (on which see 5) permitting a breach of the UK's international law obligations. After sustained criticism by many that such legislation would undermine the rule of law, the proposals were dropped.

The unwillingness of the courts to countenance the statutory exclusion of the supervisory jurisdiction of the ordinary courts is also illustrated by *R (Privacy International) v Investigatory Powers Tribunal* [2019] UKSC 22. It was argued that the Investigatory Powers Tribunal erred in law in deciding that the Secretary of State had power to issue warrants authorising the intelligence services to conduct computer hacking on a thematic basis rather than authorising specified acts in relation to specified property. Section 67(8) of the Regulation of Investigatory Powers Act 2000 provides that 'determinations, awards and other decisions of the Tribunal (including decisions as to whether they have jurisdiction) shall not be subject to appeal or be liable to be questioned in any court'. The majority of the Supreme Court held that section 67(8) only barred challenges to legally valid determinations and did not bar challenges to decisions vitiated by error of law. In the light of the reasoning in *Anisminic*, the fact that section 67(8) did not exclude 'purported determinations', as the Asylum and Immigration (Treatment of Claimants) Bill 2004 sought to do, was considered striking: see [101], [105], [109] and [165].

It is particularly significant that the court unanimously accepted that the rule of law required that there be a 'supreme interpretative and enforcing authority' which 'by its nature resides in courts of law': see Lord Sumption at [209]. But the minority (of which he was part) considered that the rule of law was sufficiently vindicated by the judicial character of the Investigatory Powers Tribunal, seeing it as a judicial body independent of the executive which exercised powers of judicial review on the same basis as the High Court: [172], [199]. They considered that there was nothing constitutionally offensive in Parliament reallocating the High Court's judicial review jurisdiction to such a tribunal.

The statutory basis of the tribunal meant that its jurisdiction and power was limited, its members originally had tenure for only five years, and there were no safeguards against reductions in their salaries. The minority did not consider that these factors, or the possibility that such a tribunal would develop a body of law that differed from the general law, affected the issue. In this they may not have given sufficient weight to the position of the High Court which Blackstone, III, chapter four 4, 41–42, described as 'the supreme court of common law in this kingdom' and as keeping all 'inferior jurisdictions within the bounds of their authority'.

*Anisminic* and the cases following it provide the foundation for the more recent views expressed by Lord Steyn and Lord Hope in *Jackson's* case (see 8–9) and by three members of the Supreme Court in *Privacy International* that the rule of law might require a court not to uphold a statutory provision which purported wholly to exclude the supervisory jurisdiction of the ordinary courts. Lord Carnwath, building on critical steps taken by the Supreme Court in *R (Cart) v Upper Tribunal* [2011] UKSC 28 at [30] in relation to the reviewability of decisions of the Upper Tribunal, considered (at [131]) that 'it is ultimately for the courts, not the legislature, to determine the limits set by the rule of law to the power to exclude review'. Two reasons support this view.

First, as noted above, even the minority in *Privacy International* accepted that the rule of law requires that there be a 'supreme interpretative and enforcing authority'. In *Cart* Laws LJ stated that 'statute law has to be mediated by an authoritative judicial source, independent both of the legislature which made the statute, the executive government which (in the usual case) procured its making, and the public body by which the statute is administered', and that only a court can fulfil that role: [2009] EWHC 3052 (Admin) at [36]. Otherwise the interpreter would be judge in its own cause 'with the ills of arbitrary government which that would entail'. Laws LJ concluded at [38] that 'if the meaning of a statutory text is not controlled by such a judicial authority, it would at length be degraded to nothing more than a matter of opinion'. In *Privacy International* Lord Lloyd-Jones (at [160]) wholeheartedly endorsed Laws LJ's 'exposition of the principle that it is a necessary corollary of the sovereignty of Parliament that there should exist an authoritative and independent body which can interpret and mediate legislation made by Parliament'.

In *Cart* Laws LJ also stated that Parliament may modify, sometimes radically, the procedures by which statute law is mediated, including by the creation of new judicial authorities which are authoritative and independent: [2009] EWHC 3052 (Admin) at [39]–[40]. This passage was relied on by the minority in *Privacy International*. But the Supreme

Court in *Cart* (at [30], [40] and [89]) considered that rule of law principles meant that the authoritative judicial source must be the High Court
because it was a court of unlimited jurisdiction and it was for the ordinary courts to decide whether the statutory provisions for the administration of justice adequately protected the rule of law.

Secondly, the very concept of continuing Parliamentary sovereignty
requires those who are entrusted with power limited by statutory language, however, broad it might be, to keep within the boundaries of
the powers prescribed by statute. As Farwell LJ stated in *R v Shoreditch
Assessment Committee, ex p Morgan* [1910] 2 KB 859, 880:

> the existence of the limit necessitates an authority to determine and enforce it:
> it is a contradiction in terms to create a tribunal with limited jurisdiction and
> unlimited power to determine such limit at its own will and pleasure – such a
> tribunal would be autocratic, not limited.

It follows that another body must determine whether executive and
administrative exercises of statutory power are faithful to the statutory
remit by interpreting it.

If there is no right of access to the courts, in reality, a principle of
parliamentary sovereignty would be replaced by a principle of executive
sovereignty. The result would be, to paraphrase Lord Atkin's Humpty
Dumpty analogy in the passage from *Liversidge v Anderson* referred to
at 142, that the statutory words used by Parliament might be taken to
mean whatever the tribunal or member of the executive relying on them
chooses them to mean. That has not been part of the UK's constitutional
arrangements since the seventeenth-century settlement.

An opportunity to test this may arise if the muscular ouster clause
in the draft Fixed-term Parliaments Act 2011 (Repeal) Bill is enacted. It
provides that a court may not question 'any decision or purported decision' relating to the prerogative powers to dissolve Parliament or the limits or extent of those powers, although it does not seek to reverse the
decision on prorogation in *Miller 2 & Cherry*, see 13 and 125.

# VI.  JUDICIAL CIRCUMSPECTION

Although it may ultimately be for the courts, not the legislature, to determine the limits set by the rule of law to the power to exclude review by
the ordinary courts, they have only contemplated this possibility in what

they have described as 'exceptional circumstances' (see 9 and 136). One commentator has described those circumstances as 'certain extreme, hypothetical situations': Hooper, at 1 and 17. Courts may also in principle be entitled to substitute their conclusions for those of the public authority on all questions of law, but, see 129–130, where the statutory language, although legally having only one meaning, is very imprecise they may be reluctant to do so. As seen from chapters five and eight, they may also abstain or show restraint where the issue is a policy matter which is more appropriately decided by the democratically elected organs of the state and is therefore an issue for Parliament and legislation rather than for the courts, or where the primary decision-maker's institutional and factual expertise on a question mean that it is better equipped than the court to make the decision.

## VII. PROTECTION OF MINORITIES UNDER THE ECHR AND THE COMMON LAW

Notwithstanding the limitations described at 63–65, it is sometimes said in judgments that the substantive rights set out in the ECHR reflect common law basic rights. Examples given include the rights to a fair trial and Article 7's provision that no one shall be held guilty of any criminal offence on account of any act or omission which did not constitute a criminal offence at the time when it was committed. Similar statements have been made about the prohibitions of torture and inhuman or degrading treatment and slavery in ECHR Articles 3 and 4.

The statement in *Duncan v Jones* that English law does not recognise any special right of public meeting can be contrasted with the invocation of the right to freedom of assembly in *DPP v Jones* [1999] 2 AC 240 as the basis for finding that peaceful protest on a highway is lawful. Moreover, soon after *Attorney-General v Guardian Newspapers Ltd (No 1)* discussed at 143, it became clear that the decision was an outlier. Lord Oliver's dissent referred to Blackstone's statement that the liberty of the press is essential to the nature of a free state. Blackstone also stated that it consisted 'in laying no *previous* restraints upon publications and not in freedom from censure for criminal matter when published': *Commentaries* IV 151.

Well before the enactment of the HRA, in *Attorney-General v Guardian Newspapers Ltd (No 2)* [1990] 1 AC 109, Lord Goff had stated that there was no difference in principle between the common law and the right to freedom of expression set out in ECHR Article 10. The basis upon which the House of Lords in *Derbyshire CC v Times Newspapers Ltd* [1993] AC 534, 550–51 held that a local authority could not as such bring an action for defamation was the fundamental right to freedom of expression in the common law. In 2002, Lord Bingham stated that 'the fundamental right of freedom of expression has been recognised at common law for very many years': *R v Shayler* [2002] UKHL 11 at [21].

The statements that the substantive rights set out in the ECHR reflect what are basic common law rights are also true of the prohibition of slavery and torture and inhumane and degrading treatment which are deeply ingrained in our system: see respectively *R v Knowles, ex p Somersett* (1772) 20 St Trials 1, and *A v Home Secretary* [2005] UKHL 71 at [11]–[12], [64]–[65], [81], [129]. They are unlawful at common law because they contravene peremptory norms of customary international law: see also *R v Bow St Metropolitan Stipendiary Magistrate, ex p Pinochet (No 3)* [2000] AC 147 at 197–99. Although of more recent origin, so is the prohibition on racial discrimination: *R (European Roma Rights Centre) v Home Secretary* [2004] UKHL 55 at [48] and [98]–[103].

That is, however, not the position for other substantive rights set out in the ECHR. In *R (Laporte) v Chief Constable of Gloucestershire* [2006] UKHL 55 at [34] Lord Bingham stated that in general 'the approach of the English common law to freedom of expression and assembly was hesitant and negative, permitting that which was not prohibited'. That and the examples at 62–63 of failures by the common law to protect privacy, and decisions limiting state surveillance, shows that it is oversimplistic to say that all the ECHR rights reflect common law basic rights. Other examples include the cases discussed in chapter five in which the Strasbourg court has held that Convention rights have been infringed while UK courts had held that there was no infringement at all, or that any infringement was justified. These suggest differing approaches to how certain statutory and common law powers and discretions must be to qualify as prescribed by law and what will justify an interference with an individual's basic rights.

Essentially, while some protection to basic substantive human rights is given by the common law right of access to the ordinary courts and the principle of legality, the interpretative approach embodied in that principle means that the protection does not prevail against sufficiently clear legislative language. Before the HRA brought Convention rights into our laws these limitations led some judges to use the language of constitutional rights in such areas, on which see 122. In *Watkins v Home Office* [2006] UKHL 17 at [64], Lord Rodger stated that 'the judges were, more or less explicitly, looking for a means of ... having the benefits of incorporation without incorporation', but that after the enactment of the HRA 'such heroic efforts are unnecessary: the Convention rights form part of our law and provide a rough equivalent of a written code of constitutional rights, albeit not one tailor-made for this country'.

It might thus appear that, apart from the right of access to the courts, the protection of the substantive rights of the minority, and the balance between basic rights of individuals and the rights and interests of others and the community, comes from the way the ECHR was brought into UK law and the way the HRA preserves Parliamentary sovereignty, rather than from the common law itself. This is particularly so in relation to the qualified rights in ECHR articles 8–11 to private and family life, and freedom of thought, conscience, religion, expression, assembly and association. These rights must be secured without discrimination on any ground such as sex, race, religion, political or other opinion, but they may be restricted by law if communal interests justify this as 'necessary in a democratic society'. For articles 8–11, the justifying interests referred to are: national security, public safety, the economic well-being of the country, the prevention of disorder or crime, the protection of health or morals and the protection of the rights or freedoms of others. Freedom of expression can also be limited to prevent the disclosure of confidential information or to maintain the authority and integrity of the judiciary.

In his Reith lectures, Lord Sumption criticised the way Parliament in enacting the HRA tied the UK to a system of law whose development was the task of the Strasbourg court, a court which is entirely outside the UK's own political institutions. He did so for three linked reasons. The first was that the way the Strasbourg court has developed the law resulted in the inclusion of rights which are unsuitable for inclusion in any human rights instrument. The second was that, although recognising that some concepts do evolve, the court's dynamic 'living instrument' approach to the interpretation of the ECHR went far beyond what is justified: Sumption, 56–58. The third was that its approach to the exceptions and qualifications to the Convention rights, that is its approach to proportionality, was flawed because where the balance between the rights and the justifying interest should lie was a matter of opinion which should generally be resolved politically through legislation rather than by the courts: Sumption, 48 and 61–63. Although Parliament clearly concluded that a specific statutory regime was needed to protect minority rights, he stated (at 61) that 'not everything that a democratic Parliament does is consistent with a democratic constitution'.

Lord Sumption considers that there are probably only two categories of rights which are truly fundamental and generally accepted in that sense. One is rights without which 'social existence is not possible'. He lists freedom from arbitrary detention and from physical injury or death; equality before the law; and recourse to impartial and independent courts. His second category is rights 'without which a community cannot function in a democracy' because 'there must at least be freedom of thought and expression, assembly and association and the right to participate on equal terms in fair and regular elections'. This seems underinclusive, omitting, for example, a right to a minimum level of education.

As to rights which are unsuitable for inclusion in any human rights instrument, Lord Sumption has stated that the important distinction is between 'interpreting existing rights in the light of current conditions and recognising new rights on the ground that, although not in the legislation, they would have been if such an instrument had been drafted in the same spirit today': Sumption in Barber, Ekins and Yowell, 216. He maintains that the Strasbourg court's dynamic approach has transformed the ECHR from an expression of noble values to something meaner by including some highly disputable questions which should be in the province of the political process rather than the law.

It must be accepted that there has been some 'mission-creep' by the Strasbourg Court, for example the application since *Al-Skeini v UK* (2011) 53 EHRR 18 of the ECHR to military operations in non-Convention countries. UK courts have expressed significant reservations about this: see for example *Serdar Mohammed v Ministry of Defence* [2015] EWCA Civ 843 [8] and [10]. But Lord Sumption's description of the interpretation of ECHR Article 8 as 'the most striking example' of this is open to question.

It is doubtful whether matters such as the legal status of children, artificial insemination, homosexuality, same-sex unions and eviction for non-payment of rent can be dismissed, as he does, as not natural implications of the right to respect for private and family life and the home. As Lady Hale observed, 'a person's sex life is surely a paradigm example of a private life' and 'the relation between parent and child lies at the heart of family life'. Moreover, Lord Sumption has recognised elsewhere, albeit tentatively, that minorities can legitimately claim protection against some laws in a democracy. He has stated that they can do so if they are identified by reference to some abiding characteristic (for example religion, ethnicity, nationality, sexual orientation) and they are placed at a permanent disadvantage under laws enacted by the majority which cannot be rectified by ordinary political processes: Sumption in Barber, Ekins and Yowell, 220–21.

In concentrating on the headline rights, he regards as 'truly fundamental' and commonly accepted, Lord Sumption does not address the difficult question of whether limitations on those rights, particularly the qualified rights in both categories, are also above political debate. While the headline rights, such as 'right to life' and 'freedom of expression', may be ones that are generally accepted, the question of where to place the limitations to them in the way that ECHR Articles 2 and 10 do, and how to balance those limitations against the rights themselves may not be so clear. Lord Sumption's reasoning gives no role to the courts in that process. Nor does he grapple with how, if the limitations and qualifications to the rights are not above political debate, the rights can be characterised as 'truly fundamental'.

For instance, he regards detention without trial as a response to political violence and terrorism in peacetime as 'morally and politically indefensible', accepts that a court can act as a check on this, and states that 'there must be access to independent judges to vindicate these rights ... and enforce the limits of state power'. To this extent he appears to accept that the right is above political debate and can be checked by a court, but he also states of indigenous common law sources of human rights that they are not secure and 'like *any* other rule of domestic law' (emphasis added) 'can be overridden by legislation'.

Another right which he recognises as truly fundamental is freedom from physical injury or death. But even the right to life is qualified. For instance, deprivation of life is not a breach of the right under ECHR Article 2 if the force used is absolutely necessary in defence against unlawful violence, to prevent the escape of a person lawfully detained or to quell a riot or insurrection. Is it only the prohibition of torture and inhumane or degrading treatment, said (see 149) to be deeply ingrained in our system, which is, as a peremptory norm of international law, the subject of an absolute prohibition? What is the status of the statutory defence in section 134(4) and (5) of the Criminal Justice

Act 1988 where a person charged with torture shows 'lawful authority, justification or excuse', and to what extent is this a matter for a court to determine rather than within the province of the political process? Would torture on the ground of the 'ticking clock' argument some use to justify it in order to obtain the information necessary to prevent the detonation of a nuclear bomb in a city centre be a matter for the courts or purely a political question? See the discussion in Levinson (ed), 2004. Other examples of difficult issues that have arisen include the intensive interrogation practices such as hooding and deprivation of sleep used in Northern Ireland (*Ireland v UK* (1978) 2 EHRR 25) or more recently the practices of the United States at its Guantánamo Bay detention camp.

What of Lord Sumption's second reason for criticising the HRA for tying the UK to a system of law whose development is entirely outside the UK's own political institutions: that the Strasbourg Court has gone much further than what is legitimate under a dynamic 'living instrument' approach to interpretation? As acknowledged above, this may sometimes be true, but it is important to note that purely domestic common law interpretation usually regards statutes as 'always speaking'. This has allowed courts to apply an updating construction so that the statute is recognised as covering circumstances which have come into existence since its enactment due to new scientific or technical knowledge or changing social attitudes: Bennion, chapter 14.

There are well recognised limits to common law dynamic interpretation: requirements of consistency with legislative intention or that a clear purpose in the legislation can only be fulfilled by such a construction, and prohibition on a meaning which is 'conceptually different' from what Parliament intended or using it to fill gaps in the legislation: *Royal College of Nursing of the United Kingdom v Department of Health and Social Security* [1981] AC 800, 822, *Oakley v Birmingham CC* [2001] 1 AC 617, 631 and *HMRC v News Corp. UK & Ireland Ltd.* [2021] EWCA Civ. 91 at [59]–[63] and [74]. But it is a well-recognised common law technique and there are many examples of it. Three will suffice.

In *Attorney General v Edison Telephone Co of London Ltd* (1880) 6 QBD 244, 254 the Telegraph Act 1869 was held to apply to telephones which had not been invented or contemplated in 1869. Secondly, *Dyson Holdings Ltd v Fox* [1976] QB 503 and *Fitzpatrick v Sterling Housing Association* [2001] 1 AC 27 illustrate how language and the scope of a common word changes to accord with changing social attitudes. They concern the entitlement, originating in a 1920 statute, of members of a statutory tenant's 'family' to succeed to the tenancy. *Dyson's* case held that the term 'family' in 1975 included unmarried partners, and *Fitzpatrick's* case that it now includes same-sex partners although neither would have been included in 1920. Thirdly, as Lord Bingham stated in *R (Quintavalle) v Secretary of State for Health* [2003] UKHL 13 'the meaning of "cruel and unusual punishments" has not changed over the years since [the Bill of Rights] 1689, but many punishments which were not then thought to fall within that category would now be held to do so'.

Lord Sumption's third reason for criticising tying our law to the Strasbourg Court concerns that court's approach to proportionality: the way in which the fundamental rights of individuals are balanced with the exceptions and qualifications to those rights which are said to be justified by the general interests of the community. This, he maintains, removes balancing decisions from the political sphere to the legal sphere and as a result he considers that UK courts have a 'growing propensity to challenge legislative and governmental decisions'. It could be said that his judgment in the *Bank Mellat* case discussed at 67 is a prime example of this but that the compelling conclusion of the dissenting justices shows that it is not a necessary consequence of Strasbourg proportionality. But, in any event, he discounts the extent to which the domestic version of proportionality discussed at 58–60 is in essence a common law concept. It is a synthesis of the principles derived from the case law of other common law Commonwealth systems as well as of European ones by the legitimate process of common law doctrinal development in the incremental way described at 43–44.

The result is that proportionality is now an important tool in the armoury of the common law for the protection of minorities. In the *UNISON* case discussed at 75–76, which Lord Sumption regards as 'perfectly orthodox', the Supreme Court applied it to common law rights of a constitutional or fundamental nature, in that case the right of access to justice: see [2017] UKSC 51 at [88]. Although the final step has not yet been taken to make domestic proportionality a completely free-standing common law principle, it is distinct from and not doctrinally dependent on the Strasbourg jurisprudence. Lord Sumption himself has questioned whether the differences between proportionality at common law and under the ECHR are in practice significant: *Pham v Home Secretary* [2015] UKSC 19 at [107]. But does that mean that for him, even in the case of the rights which he accepts are truly fundamental and commonly accepted, at common law the balancing process is a matter of opinion which should generally be resolved politically through legislation rather than by the courts? It surely should not be, although courts should be sensitive and show restraint in contexts and matters such as those discussed at 66–68 and 126–129 which are more appropriately decided by the democratic organs of the state.

The domestic version of proportionality is one of the manifestations of a new confidence in the common law roots of fundamental rights and values and their continuing vigour. Although, initially to some extent overlooked (see 150), in decisions such as *UNISON, Osborn* and *Kennedy* (see 75, 81 and 59) the Supreme Court has demonstrated an increased willingness to afford robust protection of such rights at common law. In *Kennedy*, Lord Mance stated that domestic law should be the natural starting point in any dispute and that 'in some areas, the common law may go further than the Convention': [2014] UKSC 20 at [46]. Lord Toulson agreed, stating at [113] that 'what we now term human rights law and public law has developed through our common law over a long period of time' and that 'it needs to be emphasised that it was not the purpose of the Human Rights Act that the common law should become an ossuary'.

Notwithstanding this new confidence in the common law, the discussion in this and earlier chapters shows that there remains uncertainty about the extent to which the common law can guarantee fundamental rights. The result is that at present the clearest and most direct process for reconciling the protection of the fundamental rights of individuals and minorities and the Parliamentary sovereignty which embodies the rights of majorities is the way in which the ECHR is given effect by the HRA as described in chapter one. That process creates what amounts to a partnership between the courts and Parliament. The example of the disenfranchisement of prisoners shows that, if Parliament holds out long enough, and some minor administrative changes are made, the Strasbourg institutions will accept the result so that 'consistently with our most fundamental constitutional principle, Parliament is in charge': see Hale 2019.

Is there, however, potential for protection of rights by a purely domestic common law route? This remains an important question in the light of proposals for a British Bill of Rights and a review of the HRA. These featured in the Conservative party's general election manifestos in 2015 and (more vaguely) in 2019. The areas of reform identified by the Government in evidence to the House of Lords EU Committee in

2016 concerned the weight UK courts should give to the decisions of the Strasbourg Court, the potential liability of British troops serving overseas for action undertaken in combat; and the balance between potentially conflicting rights such as freedom of expression and privacy. Arguably that had already been done in the case of the latter by sections 12 and 13 of the HRA. In relation to journalistic and literary material, section 12 requires courts to have particular regard to the importance of freedom of expression and section 13 requires them to have particular regard to the importance of freedom of thought, conscience and religion: see evidence of the Rt Hon Michael Gove MP, then the Secretary of State for Justice.

The Committee summarised the Government's two main objectives as 'to restore national faith in human rights and to give human rights a greater national identity': HL EU Committee 2016, at §3 and see at §§82–83. It criticised the feasibility and value of this because, at that time, what was proposed did not depart significantly from the rights in the ECHR. The Committee also stated that, if the British Bill of Rights provided a lower level of protection than the ECHR, the common law would be unlikely to fill the gaps.

Since then, in February 2020 the UK declined to commit to remaining in the ECHR: *The Future Relations with the EU: The UK's Approach to Negotiations* CP 2020. Two months later, in evidence to the House of Commons Committee on the Future Relationship with the EU, Mr Gove, now the Chancellor of the Duchy of Lancaster and Minister for the Cabinet Office, stated that the UK had no plans to leave the ECHR or 'to resile, or revoke or retreat' from it at all, but that the Government would not commit it to remaining because that was a question of sovereignty: HC 203, Evidence, Q223, 27 April 2020 and Q309 27 May 2020. In September 2020, although the Rt Hon Robert Buckland QC MP, the Secretary of State for Justice, stated that the UK remained fully committed to the ECHR, he also announced a further review of the HRA as part of the consideration of the balance between the rights of individuals and effective government. Established in December 2020, the review is to consider the relationship between national courts and the Strasbourg court, and the way the HRA balances the roles of courts, Government and Parliament.

There are some indications which suggest that the common law does have processes analogous to the HRA's process for reconciling the protection of the fundamental rights of individuals and minorities and Parliamentary sovereignty. They include the decision in *Anisminic* and the Parliamentary reaction to it and the more recent cases on statutory exclusion of access to the ordinary courts discussed at 144–147. They also include the still underdeveloped category of 'constitutional statutes', on which see 120–123. Common law proportionality and the circumspection shown when courts are asked to review complex polycentric policy questions which are more appropriately decided by the democratically elected organs of the state, and are therefore an issue for Parliament and legislation rather than for the courts, provide a doctrinal way forward.

The saga started by the *Anisminic* case suggests that the right of access to the ordinary courts may survive an apparently clear statutory attempt to exclude it and that Parliament's response is not necessarily to override the decision. In that case it was to accommodate the rule of law issues underlying the House of Lords' approach by the provision of an appeal to the Court of Appeal. As noted at 144–145, in a sense what happened then can be seen as a similar dialogue between court and legislature to the one contemplated when a court makes a declaration under section 4 of the HRA that a statutory provision is incompatible with ECHR rights, leaving it to Parliament to decide what to do.

Dicey contrasted the enduring power of our largely unwritten, and unentrenched, constitution with the entrenched but often short-lived constitutions of other countries. The number of changes since 1997 shows how inappropriate this comparison is today. But even in Dicey's day our constitution only appeared enduring because its foundational rule, parliamentary sovereignty, enabled all other rules to be changed at the will of those in power at any time. That, while enabling majorities in an unlimited way, does not protect minorities and thus does not resolve what has been described (see 133–134) as the great dilemma of modern democracies. A constitution must be more than 'a mere rope of sand' (the telling phrase coined in 1768 by the then Lieutenant-Governor and Chief Justice of Massachusetts and quoted by Mann 1978 at 533).

The model used in the HRA shows how weight can be given to fundamental rights and rules while retaining sovereignty and without entrenchment. The discussion above suggests that a purely domestic law route also has the potential to do this in relation to access to the ordinary courts. But, as Lord Scarman observed in *Duport Steel v Sirs* [1980] 1 WLR 142 at 169, for this to happen 'the constitution's separation of powers, or more accurately functions, must be observed'. He considered that otherwise 'society will … be ready for Parliament to cut the power of the judges' and 'their power to do justice will become more restricted by law than it need be, or is'.

# ACKNOWLEDGEMENTS

Writing a short book is in many ways more challenging than writing a long one, especially when deprived of the crutch that footnotes offer an author. I am very grateful to Nicholas McBride, the editor of this series, and Kate Whetter of Hart Publishing for giving me the chance to write on two principles of our unwritten constitution which have intrigued and puzzled me as an academic, law reformer and, most recently, a judge. They supported me calmly through the process, most of which coincided with the COVID-19 pandemic, by commenting on drafts of some of the early chapters, making books and ebooks available, and by their generous flexibility. I owe debts to many others. Emma Foubister, Hayley Hooper and Frederic Reynold read draft chapters and made perceptive comments. Richard Buxton, Lawrence Collins, Paul Craig, Timothy Endicott, Charles Haddon-Cave, Tom Hickman, Tim McEvoy, Nigel Pleming, and John Spencer were enormously helpful on particular points. The guidance of Elizabeth Wells at the Bodleian Law Library on access to electronic resources was invaluable. My wife Charlotte not only put up with me through three lockdowns but read it all. Her suggestions substantially improved clarity and culled many over-long sentences, although not as many as she wanted to. The discussion in several chapters was influenced by my 2009 Blackstone Lecture, 'Reforming an Unwritten Constitution', subsequently published in the *Law Quarterly Review*, and the origins of chapter seven are to be found in my 2004 Lionel Cohen Lecture, 'Should Judges Conduct Public Inquiries?' subsequently published in the *Israel Law Review* and the *Law Quarterly Review*, and 2017 Atkin Lecture, 'Judicial Independence: Internal and External Challenges and Opportunities'.

# ABBREVIATIONS

| | |
|---|---|
| ADR | Alternative Dispute Resolution |
| BAILII | British and Irish Legal Information Institute |
| CPR | Civil Procedure Rules |
| CPS | Crown Prosecution Service |
| CRA | Constitutional Reform Act 2005 |
| ECHR | European Convention on Human Rights |
| EU | European Union |
| HMCTS | Her Majesty's Court and Tribunal Service |
| HC | House of Commons |
| HL | House of Lords |
| HRA | Human Rights Act 1998 |
| JAC | Judicial Appointments Commission |
| LASPO | Legal Aid, Sentencing and Punishment of Offenders Act 2012 |
| MP | Member of Parliament |
| OPC | Office of Parliamentary Counsel |
| Strasbourg Court | European Court of Human Rights |
| UK | United Kingdom |

# BIBLIOGRAPHY

Adonis, A, *Making Aristocracy Work: The Peerage and the Political System in Britain, 1884–1914* (Oxford, Oxford University Press, 1993)

Ahmed, F and Perry, A, 'Constitutional Statutes' (2017) 37 *OJLS* 461

Allan, TRS, *Law, Liberty, and Justice* (Oxford, Oxford University Press, 1993)

—— *Constitutional Justice: A Liberal Theory of the Rule of Law* (Oxford, Oxford University Press, 2001)

—— *The Sovereignty of Law: Freedom, Constitution and Common Law* (Oxford, Oxford University Press, 2013)

Allen, CK, *Law in the Making* 7th edn (Oxford, Oxford University Press, 1964)

Bagehot, W, *The English Constitution* (1867, London, Fontana edition 1963)

Baker, JH, *An Introduction to English Legal History* 5th edn (Oxford, Oxford University Press, 2019)

Bangalore Principles of Judicial Conduct (2002) www.unodc.org/pdf/crime/corruption/judicial_group/Bangalore_principles.pdf

Barber, N, *The Principles of Constitutionalism* (Oxford, Oxford University Press, 2018)

Barber, NW, Ekins, R and Yowell, P, *Lord Sumption and the Limits of the Law* (London, Bloomsbury, 2016)

Beatson, J, 'Should Judges Conduct Public Inquiries?' (2004) 37 *Is L Rev* 238, (2005) 121 *LQR* 221

Beatson, J and Foubister, E, 'Public Law in the UK After Brexit' in JNE Varuhas and SW Stark (eds), *The Frontiers of Public Law* (Oxford, Hart Publishing, 2019)

*Bennion on Statutory Interpretation*, Bailey, D and Norbury (eds), 7th edn (London, LexisNexis, 2017)

Bingham, T, *The Business of Judging: Selected Essays* (Oxford, Oxford University Press, 2000)

—— 'Dicey Revisited' [2002] *Public Law* 39

—— *The Rule of Law* (London, Penguin, 2011)

Blackstone, W, *Commentaries on the Laws of England* (1765–69) Liberty Fund, Online Library of Liberty, https://oll.libertyfund.org/titles/blackstone-commentaries-on-the-laws-of-england-in-four-books-2-vols

Bogdanor, V, *The New British Constitution* (Oxford, Hart Publishing, 2009)

Briggs, M (2016) *Civil Courts Structure Review: Final Report*, www.judiciary.uk/wp-content/uploads/2016/07/civil-courts-structure-review-final-report-jul-16-final-1.pdf

Brooke, H (2015) 'The History of Judicial Independence in England and Wales' [2015] *European Human Rights Law Review* 446, originally published in *Fragile Bastion – Judicial Independence in the Nineties and Beyond* (Judicial Commission of New South Wales, 2000)

Browne-Wilkinson, N, 'The Independence of the Judiciary in the 1980s' [1988] *Public Law* 44

Burrows, A, *Thinking about Statutes: Interpretation, Interaction, Improvement* (Cambridge, Cambridge University Press, 2018)

Civil Justice Statistics Quarterly (2019) https://assets.publishing.service.gov.uk/government/uploads/system/uploads/attachment_data/file/870184/civil-justice-statistics-quarterly-Oct-Dec.pdf

Coke's Institutes of the Laws of England, Part II (1642)

Committee on Ministers' Powers (1932), Cmd 4060

Consultative Council of European Judges (2007), *Opinion on Councils for the Judiciary*, Opinion no. 10(2007), Council of Europe, Strasbourg, https://rm.coe.int/168074779b

Craig, P, *Public Law and Democracy* (Oxford, Oxford University Press, 1990)

—— 'Formal and Substantive Conceptions of the Rule of Law: An Analytical Framework' [1997] *Public Law* 467

—— '*Miller*, Structural Constitutional Review and the Limits of Prerogative Power' [2017] *Public Law* 48

Crawford, J, *Chance, Order, Change: The Course of International Law* (Leiden, Brill, 2014)

—— *Brownlie's Principles of Public International Law* 9th edn (Oxford, Oxford University Press, 2019)

Criminal Law Revision Committee (1966) *Theft and Related Offences*, 8th Report Cmnd 2977

Daintith, T and Page, A, *The Executive in the Constitution* (Oxford, Oxford University Press, 1999)

De Smith, SA, *Constitutional and Administrative Law* 5th edn (H Street and R Brazier (eds), London, Penguin, 1985)

Department for Children, Schools and Families, Guidance on Religious Education (2010) www.gov.uk/government/publications/religious-education-guidance-in-english-schools-non-statutory-guidance-2010

Department for Education, Statutory guidance publications, www.gov.uk/government/collections/statutory-guidance-schools

Devlin, P, *Trial by Jury* (London, Stevens, 1956)

Dicey, AV (1885) *Introduction to the Law of the Constitution* 10th edn with introduction by ECS Wade (London, Macmillan, 1964)

—— *A Leap in the Dark: A Criticism of the Principles of Home Rule as Illustrated in the Bill of 1893* (London, John Murray, 1911).

Dickson, B, *Human Rights and the United Kingdom Supreme Court* (Oxford, Oxford University Press, 2013)

Dworkin, R, *A Matter of Principle* (Cambridge MA, Harvard University Press, 1985)

Eisenberg, M, *The Nature of the Common Law* (Cambridge MA, Harvard University Press, 1988)

Elliott, M, 'The Supreme Court's Judgment in *Miller:* In Search of Constitutional Principle' (2017) 76 *CLJ* 257

Elliott, M and Hughes, K (eds), *Common Law Constitutional Rights* (Oxford, Hart Publishing, 2020)

Endicott, T, 'Questions of Law' (1998) 114 *LQR* 292

—— *Vagueness in Law* (Oxford, Oxford University Press, 2000)

—— 'Lord Reed's Dissent in Gina Miller's case and the Principles of our Constitution' (2016/17) 8 *UKSC Yearbook* 259

Ewing, KD and Gearty, CA, *The Struggle for Civil Liberties: Political Freedom and the Rule of Law in Britain, 1914–1945* (Oxford, Oxford University Press, 2000)

Feldman, D, 'The Nature and Significance of Constitutional Legislation' (2013) 129 *LQR* 342

Finnis, J, *Natural Law and Natural Rights* (Oxford, Oxford University Press, 1980)

Fouzder, M, 'Falconer: My "Regret" Over Labour's Effort to Curb Legal Aid Budget' (2019) *Law Society Gazette* (31 May 2019)

Framework Document, *HM Court Service Framework Document* (2008) Cm 7350

Free Movement Blog, www.freemovement.org.uk/home-office-tries-to-lean-on-judges-deciding-immigration-bail-cases/ (2020)

Friedmann, W, *Legal Theory* (London, Stevens & Sons, 1967)

Fuller, L, 'Positivism and Fidelity to Law: A Reply to Hart' (1958) 71 *Harvard Law Review* 630

Galligan, DJ, *Due Process and Fair Procedures* (Oxford, Oxford University Press, 1996)

Gee, G, Hazell, R, Malleson, K and O'Brien, P, *The Politics of Judicial Independence in the UK's Changing Constitution* (Cambridge, Cambridge University Press, 2015)

Genn, H, *Paths to Justice: What People Do and Think about Going to Law* (Oxford, Hart Publishing, 1999)

—— *Judging Civil Justice* (Cambridge, Cambridge University Press, 2010)

Goff, R, 'The Search for Principle' (1984) 69 *Proc British Academy* 285, reprinted as an Appendix to W Swadling and G Jones (eds), *The Search for Principle* (Oxford, Oxford University Press, 1999)

Goldsworthy, J, *Parliamentary Sovereignty: Contemporary Debates* (Cambridge, Cambridge University Press, 2010)

Goudkamp, J, 'Restating the Common Law? The Social Action, Responsibility and Heroism Act 2015' (2017) 37 *Legal Studies* 577

Greenberg, D, 'Dangerous Trends in Modern Legislation' [2015] *Public Law* 96

Hailsham, Q, *Hamlyn Revisited: The British Legal System Today* (London, Stevens & Sons, 1983)

Hale, B, 'Law and Politics: A Reply to Reith' (2019) 24 *Judicial Review* 205

Hart, HLA, *The Concept of Law* (Oxford, Oxford University Press, 1961)

Haldane, RB, *An Autobiography* (London, Hodder & Stoughton, 1929)

Henderson, E, *Foundations of English Administrative Law* (Cambridge MA, Harvard University Press, 1963)

Hennessy, P, *The Hidden Wiring: Unearthing the British Constitution* (London, Victor Gollancz, 1995)

Heydon, JD, 'Threats to Judicial Independence: The Enemy Within' (2013) 129 *LQR* 205

Hickman, TR, 'In Defence of the Legal Constitution' (2005) 55 *University of Toronto Law Journal* 981

Hobbes, T, *De Cive, The English Version* (1647, Warrender, H (ed), Oxford, Oxford University Press, 1983)

—— *Leviathan* (1651, Tuck, R (ed), Cambridge Texts in the History of Political Thought, Cambridge, Cambridge University Press, 1991)

Hoffmann, L, 'The Universality of Human Rights' (2009) 125 *LQR* 416

—— 'Separation of Powers' [2002] *Judicial Review* 137

Hooper, HJ, 'Legality, Legitimacy and Legislation: The Role of Exceptional Circumstances in Common Law Judicial Review' (2021) 41 *OJLS* forthcoming, page references are to the advance article published online 3 December 2020: https://doi.org/10.1093/ojls/gqaa041

House of Commons Constitutional Affairs Committee (2004) Judicial Appointments and Supreme Court (court of final appeal) 1st report of Session 2003-04 HC 48-I

House of Commons Justice Committee (2019) Court and Tribunal reforms, 2nd report of Session 2019

—— (2020) *Coronavirus (COVID-19): The impact on courts*, 6th report of Session 2019–21

House of Commons Library Briefing Paper (2019) *Acts and Statutory Instruments: the volume of UK legislation 1850–2019* CBP 7438 by Philip Loft

—— (2019A) *UK Election Statistics 1918–2019: A Century of Elections*, CBP 7529 by Lukas Audickas, Richard Cracknell and Philip Loft

House of Lords Committee on the Inquiries Act 2005 (2014), Session 2013–14 *The Inquiries Act 2005: Post-legislative scrutiny* HL 143

House of Lords EU Committee (2016), 12th Report 2015–16, HL Paper 139, 9 May 2016

House of Lords Constitution Committee (2006) 5th Report of Session 2005–06, *Constitutional Reform Act 2005*, HL Paper 83

—— (2006–07) 6th Report of Session 2006–07, *Relations between the Executive, the Judiciary and Parliament*, HL Paper 151

—— (2010) 6th Report of Session 2010–11, *Public Bodies Bill*, HL Paper 43

—— (2017A) 4th Report of Session 2017–19, *Preparing Legislation for Parliament*, HL Paper 27

—— (2017B) 7th Report of Session 2017–19, *Judicial Appointments; follow-up*, HL Paper 32

—— (2018) 16th Report of Session 2017–19, *The Legislative Process: The Delegation of Powers*, HL Paper 225

House of Lords and House of Commons, Joint Committee on Human Rights (2006–07), 19th Report, *Counter-Terrorism policy and Human Rights*, HL Paper 60/HC 394

Hutton Report, (2004) *Report of the Inquiry into the Circumstances Surrounding the Death of Dr David Kelly CMG* HC 247, https://fas.org/irp/world/uk/huttonreport.pdf (accessed 24 September 2020)

Jackson, Sir Rupert (2009) *Review of Civil Litigation Costs: Final Report*, The Stationary Office, December 2009, www.judiciary.uk/wp-content/uploads/JCO/Documents/Reports/jackson-final-report-140110.pdf (accessed 24 September 2020)

—— (2015) *Confronting Costs Management*, Harbour Lecture May 2015 www.judiciary.uk/wp-content/uploads/2015/05/speech-jackson-lj-confronting-costs-management-1.pdf (accessed 24 September 2020)

Jennings, I, *The Law and the Constitution* 3rd and 5th edns (London, University of London Press, 1938 and 1959)

Johnson, N, *Reshaping the British Constitution: Essays in Political Interpretation* (Basingstoke, Palgrave Macmillan, 2004)

Judicial Power Project, see https://judicialpowerproject.org.uk

Juratowitch, B, *Retroactivity and the Common Law* (Oxford, Hart Publishing, 2008)

Justice and Security Green Paper (2011) Cm 8194 https://assets.publishing.service.gov.uk/government/uploads/system/uploads/attachment_data/file/79293/green-paper_1.pdf (accessed 24 September 2020)

Knight, CJS, 'The Rule of Law, Parliamentary Sovereignty and the Ministerial Veto' (2015) 131 *LQR* 547

Latimer House Principles (2003), *Commonwealth (Latimer House) Principles on the Accountability of and the Relationship between the Three Branches of Government* (Commonwealth Secretariat) www.cpahq.org/cpahq/cpadocs/Commonwealth%20Latimer%20Principles%20web%20version.pdf (accessed 14 September 2020)

Law Commission, *A Criminal Code for England and Wales* Law Com No 177 (1989)

—— *Legislating the Criminal Code: Offences against the Person and General Principles; A Consultation Paper* Law Com CP No 122 (1992)

—— *Binding Over* Law Com No 222 (1994)

—— *The Sentencing Code* Law Com No 382 HC Paper 1724 (2018)

—— *Simplification of the Immigration Rules Consultation Paper* CP 242 (2019)

—— *Simplification of the Immigration Rules* Law Com No 388 (2020)

Laws, J, 'The Constitution: Morals and Rights' [1996] PL 622

—— *The Constitutional Balance*, (Oxford, Hart Publishing 2021).

Leggatt, Sir Andrew (2001) *Tribunals for Users: One System, One Service*, Dept. for Constitutional Affairs

Leveson, Sir Brian (2012) *An Inquiry into the culture, practices and ethics of the British Press* HC 780-i to iv

—— Evidence to House of Commons Culture, Media and Sport Committee *Regulation of the Press* HC 143-iv, 10 October 2013

Levinson, S (ed), *Torture: A Collection* (Oxford, Oxford University Press, 2004)

Locke, J, *Second Treatise of Civil Governance* (1690)

Loughlin, M (1992) *Public Law and Political Theory* (Oxford, Oxford University Press, 1992)

—— *The British Constitution: A Very Short Introduction* (Oxford, Oxford University Press, 2013)

Macpherson Report (1999), *Report of the Stephen Lawrence Inquiry* Cm. 4262

Mann, FA, 'Britain's Bill of Rights' (1978) 94 *LQR* 512

Mann, FA, *Foreign Affairs in English Courts* (Oxford, Oxford University Press, 1986)

Milsom, SFC, *Historical foundations of the Common Law* (London, Butterworths, 1969)

Montesquieu, *De l'Esprit des Lois* (1748)

Moore-Bick Report, *Grenfell Tower Inquiry: Phase 1 Report* October 2019

Mulcahy, L, 'The Possibilities and Desirability of Mediator Neutrality: Towards an Ethics of Partiality (2001) 10 *Social and Legal Studies* 505

Mulheron, R, 'Legislating Dangerously: Bad Samaritans, Good Society, and the Heroism Act 2015' (2017) 80 *MLR* 88

Olowofoyeku, A, *Suing Judges* (Oxford, Oxford University Press, 1993)

Office of the Parliamentary Counsel (OPC) (2013A) *When laws become too complex*, 16 April 2013, www.gov.uk/government/publications/when-laws-become-too-complex/when-laws-become-too-complex

—— (2013B) *Good law principles, current challenges and what the Office of the Parliamentary Counsel are doing to promote good law*, 16 April 2013, www.gov.uk/guidance/good-law

O'Nions, 'Fat Cat Lawyers and "Illegal" Migrants: the Impact of Intersecting Hostilities and Toxic Narratives on Access to Justice' (2019) 42 *Journal of Social Welfare and Family Law* 319, www.tandfonline.com/doi/full/10.1080/0964906 9.2020.1796222?af=R (accessed 7 October 2020)

Plato, *The Statesman*, trans Annas & Waterfield, Cambridge Texts in the History of Political Thought, 360BC, Cambridge, Cambridge University Press, 1995)

Pollock, Sir Frederick, 'A Plea for Historical Interpretation' (1923) 39 *LQR* 163

Public Law Project, (2018) *The Digitalisation of Tribunals: What we know and what we need to know*, https://publiclawproject.org.uk/wp-content/uploads/2018/04/The-Digitalisation-of-Tribunals-for-website.pdf

Radcliffe, CJ, (1951) *The Problem of Power* (lectures given in 1951, published London, Secker & Warburg, 1952; London, Comet Books, 1958)

Rawls, J, *A Theory of Justice* (Oxford, Oxford University Press, 1972)

Raz, J, *The Authority of Law* (Oxford, Oxford University Press, 1977)

—— 'The Rule of Law and its Virtue' (1977) 93 *LQR* 195 reprinted in *The Authority of Law* (Oxford, Oxford University Press, 1979)

Renton Committee, *The Preparation of Legislation* (1975) Cmnd 6053

Reynold, F, *High Principle, Low Politics, and the Emergence of the Supreme Court* (London, Wildy, Simmonds and Hill Publishing, 2019)

Robson, W, *Justice and Administrative Law* 3rd edn (London, Stevens, 1951) (1st edn London, Macmillan, 1928)

Rozenberg, J, *Enemies of the People? How Judges Shape Society* (Bristol, Bristol University Press, 2020)

Sales, P, 'Rationality, Proportionality and the Development of the Law' (2013) 129 *LQR* 223

—— 'Rights and Fundamental Rights in English Law' (2016) 75 *CLJ* 86

—— 'The Contribution of Legislative Drafting to the Rule of Law' (2018) 77 *CLJ* 630

Sandhurst, G and Speight, A, 'Pardonable in the Heat of Crisis – But We Must Return to the Rule of Law' (Society of Conservative Lawyers, 4 April 2020)

Scarman Report, (1986) *The Brixton Disorders 10–12 April 1981* Cmnd 8427, also Pelican edition

Scott Report, (1996) *Inquiry into the Export of Defence Equipment and Dual-Use Goods to Iraq & Related Prosecutions* Cm 115

Sedley, S, *Ashes and Sparks: on Law and Justice* (Cambridge, Cambridge University Press, 2011)

Sedley, S, *Lions under the Throne: The History of Public Law* (Cambridge, Cambridge University Press, 2015)

Shklar, J, 'Political Theory and the Rule of Law' in A Hutchinson and P Monahan (eds), *The Rule of Law: Ideal or Ideology* (Toronto, Carswell, 1987)

Shetreet, S and Turenne, S, *Judges on Trial: The Independence and Accountability of the English Judiciary* 2nd edn (Cambridge, Cambridge University Press, 2013)

Simonsen, N, 'Introductory Note to Belhaj v Straw and Rahmatullah (No 1) v Ministry of Defence' (2017) 56 *International Legal Materials* 951

Simester, A and Sullivan G, *Simester and Sullivan's Criminal Law Theory and Doctrine* 7th edn (A Simester, JR Spencer, F Stark, G Sullivan and G Virgo (eds), Oxford, Hart Publishing, 2019)

Simpson, AWB, *Human Rights and the End of Empire: Britain and the Genesis of the European Convention,* (Oxford, Oxford University Press, 2004)

Smith, E, 'Acts of State in Belhaj and Rahmatullah' (2018) 134 *LQR* 20

Spencer, JR, *Hearsay Evidence in Criminal Proceedings* 2nd edn (Oxford, Hart Publishing, 2014)

—— 'The Drafting of Criminal Legislation: Need it be so Impenetrable?' [2008] *CLJ* 585.

Stevens, R, *Law and Politics: The House of Lords as a Judicial Body 1800–1976* (Chapel Hill NC, University of North Carolina Press, 1978)

—— *The English Judges: Their Role in the Changing Constitution* (Oxford, Hart Publishing, 2002)

Steyn, J, 'The Intractable Problem of the Interpretation of Legal Texts' (2003) 25 *Sydney Law Review* 5

—— 'Democracy, the Rule of Law and the Role of Judges' [2006] *European Human Rights Law Review* 243

Sumption, J, *Trials of the State: Law and the Decline of Politics* (London, Profile Books, 2019)

Susskind, R, *The End of Lawyers: Rethinking the Nature of Legal Services* (Oxford, Oxford University Press, 2008)

—— *Online Courts and the Future of Justice* (Oxford, Oxford University Press, 2019)

—— 'The Future of Courts' (2020) vol 6 The Practice, Harvard Law School Centre on the Legal Profession.

Tananaha, B, *On the Rule of Law* (Cambridge, Cambridge University Press, 2000)

Thomas, RJL (2017A) *The Judiciary within the State – Governance and Cohesion of the Judiciary*, Lionel Cohen Lecture Jerusalem, (2018) 51 *Israel Law Review* 127 www.judiciary.uk/wp-content/uploads/2017/05/lcj-lionel-cohen-lecture-20170515.pdf (accessed 24 September 2020)

—— (2017B) *The Judiciary within the State – The relationship between the branches of the State*, Michael Ryle Memorial Lecture, 15 June 2017, www.judiciary.uk/wp-content/uploads/2017/06/lcj-michael-ryle-memorial-lecture-20170616.pdf (accessed 24 September 2020)

Tomkins, A and Scott, P (eds), *Entick v Carrington: 250 Years of the Rule of Law* (Oxford, Hart Publishing, 2015)

Unger, R, *Law in Modern Society* (London, Simon and Shuster, 1976)

Venice Commission (2010), Report on the Independence of the Judicial System Part I: The Independence of the Judiciary

Vile Constitutionalism and the Separation of Powers 1967

Wade, HWR and Forsyth, C, *Administrative Law* 11th edn (Oxford, Oxford University Press, 2014)

Waldron, J, 'The Rule of Law', *The Stanford Encyclopedia of Philosophy* (Summer 2020 Edition), Edward N Zalta (ed), https://plato.stanford.edu/archives/sum2020/entries/rule-of-law/

Williams, G, *The Proof of Guilt: A Study of the English Criminal Trial* 3rd edn (London, Stevens, 1963)

Woodhouse, D, 'Modernising the Constitution: Completing the Unfinished Business' in G Canivet, M Andenas and D Fairgrieve (eds), *Independence, Accountability, and the Judiciary* (London, BIICL, 2006)

Woolf, H, *Access to Justice: Final Report to the Lord Chancellor on the Civil Justice System in England and Wales* (1996)

Wright, R, 'Liberty and the Common Law' (1945–47) 9 *Cambridge Law Journal* 2

Wright, T, *Citizens and Subjects* (London, Routledge, 1993)

UN Basic Principles on the Independence of the Judiciary, GA Resolutions 40/32 and 40/146 (1985), www.icj.org/wp-content/uploads/2014/03/UN-Basic-principles-independence-judiciary-1985-eng.pdf

UN Universal Declaration of Human Rights (1948), www.ohchr.org/EN/UDHR/Documents/UDHR_Translations/eng.pdf

UN 'What is the Rule of Law?' www.un.org/ruleoflaw/what-is-the-rule-of-law/- (accessed 13 December 2020)

Zuckerman, A, *Zuckerman on Civil Procedure: Principles of Practice* 3rd edn (London, Thomson Reuters, 2013)

# TABLE OF CASES

# TABLE OF STATUTES